CANTON ELEGY

CANTON ELEGY

A Father's Letter of Sacrifice, Survival and Love

Stephen Jin-Nom Lee
& Howard Webster

WATKINS PUBLISHING
LONDON

This edition first published in the UK and USA 2013 by
Watkins Publishing Limited, Sixth Floor,
75 Wells Street, London W1T 3QH

A member of Osprey Group

Osprey Publishing
PO Box 3985
New York, NY 10185-3985

1 3 5 7 9 10 8 6 4 2

Designed by Clare Thorpe

Printed and bound in China

A CIP record for this book is available from the British Library

ISBN: 978-1-78028-573-3

www.watkinspublishing.co.uk

AUTHOR'S NOTE

Names, places, events and dates have been changed and fictionalized at the author's discretion for dramatization and to protect the privacy of those mentioned in the book.

CONTENTS

LIST OF ILLUSTRATIONS

LIST OF PLATES

TO THE DRAGON
AND THE PHOENIX

PREFACE

On July 20, 2011, Frederick Stephen Webster and Alexandra Bo King Webster were born at the Chelsea and Westminster Hospital in London. My wife, Julianne Lee, and I named the twins after my paternal grandfather, Frederick Alexander Webster, and her paternal grandparents, Stephen Jin-Nom Lee and Belle Bo-King Lee.

Being on maternity leave, Julianne was keen to take the twins back to California that Christmas to introduce them to her family. In Chinese families twins are very lucky, even more so if they are a boy and a girl. These are called Dragon and Phoenix twins: the boy is the Dragon and the girl is the Phoenix. The Dragon represents power and the Phoenix represents luck.

It was when I was in California that Christmas with the twins that I first read the manuscript that later became this book. I knew within the first few lines that it was special. Stephen Jin-Nom Lee's manuscript had sat in a box since 1955. Here was a man who had been dead for over forty years, writing for a time in the future when his own children would be facing the end of their own lives. He had wanted to leave a legacy behind that would provide them with the comfort and certainty that, as they faced that ultimate question, they were still loved by their father. One phrase leapt from Stephen's opening letter that hit me particularly hard: "*I want my heart to have a voice so I can love you louder.*" *Canton Elegy* was his heart's voice.

With his words ringing in my head, I went and sat by the cots in the back bedroom where my own little Dragon and Phoenix were sleeping. I am in my forties, and as they slept I could scarcely imagine a time in the future when I would not be around to watch over them; that one day they would face a world alone without their father at their shoulder to guide them and keep them safe. The thought of them as elderly people, facing the end of their own lives alone and maybe afraid, broke my heart.

Stephen's words summed up everything I was feeling as a new father. That is why it suddenly became very important to me to help Stephen complete his book and see it become the legacy he always dreamt it could be. As I worked on the manuscript, the emerging book began to assume a new importance to me that I hadn't expected when I first started. Through it, I realized, I could also talk to my own children in a future time I would not see. My very own message in a bottle, containing an evergreen fragment of a father's heart untainted by old age and the decades to come that will undoubtedly separate him from his son and daughter. A place where, if they feel doubt or fear, they can journey to and listen to a blend of their father's and great-grandfather's words and find comfort, inspiration and courage. A letter sent across time to them to let them know that they are and will always be loved by their father. An assurance that not even time or space can alter.

Canton Elegy is a lasting testament to a man's heart. Stephen Lee's story *is* a great story, and the love he left behind is his greatest legacy.

Howard Webster, 2013

PROLOGUE

February 19, 1955

Dear Amy, Huey, Rudy and Yvonne,

This must come as a shock to the four of you, a letter from the Old Man sent from across the years. When you read this, you will be older than I am today, and the world you all live in will be one that I could barely recognize. Yet I believe there are constants that will never change, and one of those constants is the love that a father has for his children. As you came into this world, it was Mother who took care of you, and like many men of my generation I was conditioned to be just the breadwinner, doing my best to fulfill the duty of a father by being a provider. I have always been awkward and have certainly made many mistakes. I sometimes wonder whether I told you enough just how much you all meant to me.

That is why this letter and the pages of this manuscript are so important to me: a little reminder of a time in your life when you were all very small and we all lived together under one roof as a family; something that will make you understand the quiet, watchful love I had for you all. Many times, during our years together, I wondered if you understood me, or even if I understood you. I have often wondered if I loved you enough. You see, as you entered our lives and we became a family, I thought you would all be more dependent on your mother and me than you proved to be. All fathers know their children will one day grow up, but not one father I know is ever prepared for that day. I know that I wasn't prepared to lose my own little ones so quickly to your friends, your school, and then the world.

Amy, Huey, Rudy, Yvonne—my children.

Now that the years have rushed away with cruel speed I want *my* heart to have a voice so I can love you louder. A father's hand that can reach out across time and into a future where I will just be a memory, a hand that you can always take hold of, one that loves you still. The story you are about to read will have to make do for the conversations we never had.

There is nothing more that I can say, *my* children, except to thank God for the loan of four souls that were given into my care. It is the love I had for my children that made me a man. Good night and God bless you all until a time that waits beyond that unknown and certain far horizon, when we will all sit together, under one roof as a family again, and share stories about the lives we led and the people we became. Until we reach that far horizon, I will simply close my eyes and remember, my heart keenly reaching out into the past where I can once again hear the sound of my children's laughter.

Dad

1

LEAVING DAI WAAN

My earliest memories of my home village are the hill it stood beneath and the well-tilled fields that surrounded it, soaked in bright spring sunlight. Dai Waan was an ancient Chinese village that, in my childhood, commanded views across open countryside and the crystal-sharp breezes that swept down the valley towards it. These chill gusts could, on occasion, penetrate even the thickest of down jackets. As children, we were told bedtime stories that these breezes belonged to the ghosts of our ancestors passing through the village—echoes of the dead revisiting the footpaths and roadways of a distantly remembered life before returning to a destination that no living eye was allowed to see.

In my six-year-old memory the sky in Dai Waan was always the deepest of blues, and beneath this canopy of azure silk stood the village houses, huts and villas, while nearby, a slow-moving river snaked past our dwellings, bringing its lifeblood to our crops.

It was in this setting, on an especially hot afternoon in the summer of 1908, that I first saw a procession of burly country men emerge through the shimmering haze of the sun. They were straining under the weight of foreign-made trunks, leather suitcases and heavy crates. I could see that some of the crates were filled to the brim with green apples. As the procession neared me, their shadows stretched out before them like a parade of dark giants from a shadow puppet play, and at their head was my grandfather, returning to China after a long absence in America. The sight was magical. I got up and rushed back home to tell my grandmother.

Back at our house, my grandmother had already been alerted by telegram, and she was rushing around getting everything ready. I was banned from the house while she made sure it was tidy and told to go and wait in the courtyard. Sitting there, I could smell the delicious spices and aromas of the banquet that was being prepared under my mother's direction in the kitchen. There was to be a feast that night in honor of my grandfather's return.

Later that day I remember sitting on a small wooden bench in the kitchen with Little Uncle. We had been allowed back in and dressed in our finest clothes, and both of us were under strict instructions from Grandmother not to move and not to interfere with anything while the banquet was readied.

"The Old Man is resting and will come to see you soon," she said with a withering glare. "I want you to sit quietly, and don't start a fight with each other when he arrives."

Little Uncle was the youngest son of my grandparents and only two months older than me. Even though we became good friends in later life, at that time Little Uncle and I were not always on the best of terms. My own father had died a few years before; he had been kidnapped by bandits, then released after the ransom was paid, but died shortly afterwards of a fever contracted during his captivity. With Grandfather away in America, Little Uncle and I were the two princes vying for attention in a kingdom of women ruled over by my grandmother first and my mother second.

As we fidgeted there on the wooden bench with nothing else to do but tease each other, Little Uncle decided that it was time to play his trump card regarding my status in the family.

"Listen, the Old Man is *my* papa, but you have to call him Grandpa. He is going to bring me lots of toys, candies and American storybooks. *You* are not going to get a thing, see?"

My grandmother overheard the conversation and intervened. "Now, now, don't start," she reproved Little Uncle, threatening to slap him with the back of her hand. That made Little Uncle shut up. "Both of you will share equally any presents the Old Man brings back."

A crowd of villagers had gathered around the house when

my grandfather, a short, stout and benign-looking gentleman, finally made his grand entrance. "Papa!" shouted Little Uncle, shoving me behind him just to make sure that he would be the first in line to be greeted. I muttered, "Grandpa!" not expecting a reaction. Without a father of my own to tell me otherwise, I had always believed myself to be second best in the family. Standing there, hearing Little Uncle call out the name Papa, made me feel as alone and unworthy as I'd ever felt in my short life.

"Halloo there," the Old Man smiled. "I am glad to see you all. I have brought back some nice things for you. Ah-Nom-Moo will give them to you as soon as the boxes are opened."

Ah-Nom-Moo was the family's private name for my mother. She was a beautiful, reserved and graceful young lady who hid her smile and eager laughter from everyone but me. She was busy unpacking all the American-made bags and trunks in front of the crowd of curious neighbors who had gathered around the Lee family home. It seemed that the whole village had turned up. The Old Man, seeing the commotion his arrival had caused, directed Ah-Nom-Moo to distribute a small present to each and every man, woman and child in the gathered crowd. Then, finally, he walked over to Little Uncle and me, proudly carrying two big parcels wrapped in brightly colored paper.

"Here is yours, Ah Nom," said the Old Man, talking to me, his grandson. "And this is yours, Ah Chuan," said the Old Man to his son.

The house in Dai Waan

I had not been overlooked; I had even been accorded the small honor of receiving my gift first in memory of my late father. I don't know which mattered more, the gift or this gesture. I loved my grandpa.

As the evening banquet began, with course after course of delicious food served by the household staff, my grandfather called silence. He wanted to speak. Looking at my grandmother directly, he revealed his true reason for returning to China. He intended to take Little Uncle and me back to America to be educated. I remember how upset my grandmother looked at this news. She was afraid for us and thought we were far too young to be so far away from her care. My grandfather dismissed her concerns with a wave of his hand.

"I will take care of them, and besides, when they are in America, they can easily learn to take care of themselves. America is different, you know?"

It went without saying that my mother would not be coming with me. Her place, as a widow, was to work in my grandmother's household, to serve and to obey her husband's parents. There were few options for women like her in China in those times. Thinking back, I can see that this news must have hit her doubly hard; I was her whole world. Yet widowhood had forced her to deal in practicalities. Seeing what an opportunity it would be for me, she put her own needs aside and quietly supported my grandfather's wishes despite my grandmother's resistance. She believed that an education in America would mean that her son could become financially independent one day, never having to serve or rely on anyone else for a single thing, something she had never had. As the heated debate between my grandparents at the dinner table went on, my mother remained silent until the moment was right to speak out in support of my grandfather.

"If Grandpa should be willing to take the children to America and educate them there, I am sure Grandmother would be proud of the young men they would become, and I would always be grateful."

"But who is going to take care of me in my old age when the children are gone?" said Grandmother.

"I shall continue to devote my life at your command as long as I live, Grandmother."

And with that one sentence my mother bartered her future for mine. That night it was agreed that two little boys should be allowed to go to America with their grandfather.

A few months later my grandfather set out for America again, without us. He promised to send word when the time was right for Little Uncle and me to join him there.

Four years came and went and Little Uncle and I had ceased to believe that my grandfather would ever send for us. We were settled into a daily routine of our own, attending a school in the quiet town of Shek-Ki in Guangdong province, when the letter finally arrived. It was finally time for us to leave home forever.

This letter came as quite a shock to us both. I was nine years old, and the day after my grandmother told us the news, I remember walking with Little Uncle through the town of Shek-Ki, listening, as if from a great distance, to the casual chatter of the old men sitting at the roadside on old boxes playing mahjong. I was watching a day-to-day ritual of life that I thought would last forever, a life that I would no longer be a part of. The mahjong players were too absorbed by the dice being rolled to notice me staring at them, trying to remember everything I could about this scene. The old men would not miss me when I was many thousands of miles away, but I would miss them and the sounds of carved tiles being clicked and stacked eighteen high on a small wooden table forever. This was all I knew.

As a child, you don't really have a concept of loss: not until you experience it do you truly know what it means. I had lived with the loss of a father nearly all my young life and knew what it meant, the isolation and the overwhelming feeling of being abandoned. I was especially sad to leave my mother; she was all I had, the only thing in my childhood universe that was completely mine. And my mother, guessing how I must have been feeling, was brave, reassuring and strong. She never showed me how she truly felt. She never told me how much it cost her to let her only child go, knowing that she might never see me again.

A distant cousin, Uncle Lee Poi Fun, who was returning to America himself, would be given the task of traveling with us across the ocean and acting as our guardian. On the day we left for America, my mother dressed Little Uncle and me in our best clothes and prepared me as best she could for a future a child could hardly imagine. It was the last time she would ever comb my hair and wash my face. As I stood on the road outside the only home I had ever known, staring down at my feet and kicking dirt, my mother stood next to me holding my luggage. She put down the suitcase and knelt down close to me. I stood staring at her, unable to find any words to say. She also seemed to be seeking for something to say, something that ought to be said, but she too struggled for words. I looked back down at the dirt scratches I had made.

"You are all I have, Ah Nom. You must work hard and study hard when you arrive in America. You must also look after yourself and obey all the elders there. Remember you are fatherless and you must see your own way through and try not to depend too much on others. Grandpa loves you, yes, but he has his own problems. And your Uncle Tay, whom you will meet in America for the first time, he will do all he can to help you, but he has his own family to care for and a farm to run. The only person you can rely upon is yourself. Mummy will always love you, Ah Nom, but I will be far away. I want to be with you, but I have to stay here to give you the chance of a better life."

Looking up from the marks I had been carving in the dirt with the heel of my shoe, I finally saw how much it hurt my mother: this moment. I wanted to comfort her. To tell her everything would be fine. I was still very young, yet, understanding something of what her life would be without me, I wanted to make her feel better. But I knew nothing that I could say or do would matter. It was at that moment the child left his true childhood behind. To see the fragility upon which the lives of those we love are built and how powerless we sometimes are to make the world a better place for them, to understand that we are, ultimately, all at the mercy of our hearts—my eyes welled up with tears and I began to cry.

Seeing this, my mother pulled me to her and held me tight, barely able to hold down the deeply wrought emotion she had trained so long to bury. She whispered in my ear, her own voice breaking, "You needn't worry about me, Ah Nom. I can get along all right. I only hope that you will come back some day and then I shall be the happiest woman on earth."

Without either of us saying another word, my mother walked with me across the river that ran near our village. She stood at the roadside and kept her eyes locked on mine, as I kept mine on hers, both trying to consign every breath of the one we loved to memory.

Little Uncle had already clambered aboard the ox-drawn cart with his suitcase and was waiting for me, sitting with his back against the side of the seatless cart, staring at the tattered cloth canopy fluttering above him. My grandmother had said her goodbyes to him at the house and let one of the servants see him off. He was crying.

I slid my case next to Little Uncle's on the rough wooden floor, stained and worn with years of transporting farm produce. I hopped up onto the back of the cart and sat on my suitcase. The cart driver, seeing I was aboard, flicked his whip, and the two oxen grunted and snorted and pulled the rickety cart down the dirt track. As we drew away and my mother faded from sight, the realization finally hit me. I was on my own.

2

FIRST-CLASS CONGEE

We waited in Hong Kong for a week while our visas were processed. Then, on September 13, 1913, with our paperwork complete, I saw the SS *Persia* for the first time. The large ocean liner was a marvel. The biggest boats I had ever seen were heavily laden Chinese tow-boats being pulled upstream on the river by oxen; in places where it was impossible for animals to venture, teams of laborers called trackers would take their place. Being harnessed to a tow-boat could be dangerous and back-breaking work. Many trackers risked serious injury or even death if they stumbled or fell from the broken and treacherous paths that lined steep riverbanks as they navigated rapids and mountain passes. Life and human labor was cheap and in plentiful supply. There was never a shortage of desperate men who would risk their lives to earn a few coins to buy their children rice.

Stepping on board this huge steamship with smoke billowing from its monstrous chimneystacks, I could scarcely believe that it would float, let alone sail all the way to America. As the *Persia* left Hong Kong, I stood on the deck with Uncle Poi Fun watching the Chinese coastline fade away. Uncle Poi Fun was wearing a Western-style business suit that a tailor in Hong Kong had made for him especially for the trip. Behind us in First Class, rich Westerners were gaily chatting and laughing. Below us, milling around on the lower decks in Third Class, we could see people dressed in traditional Chinese coats and pants, all of them heading for a new world. Feeling more at home with the people in Third Class than the loud foreigners on the upper deck, I tried to go down to the lower deck.

"Hey, you can't go downstairs," said Uncle Poi Fun.

"Why not?"

"We are in First Class, idiot," said Little Uncle. He was not much older than me, yet he seemed to know far more. "First Class passengers are not allowed to go down to the Third Class deck and Third Class passengers are not allowed to come up to our First Class deck." He looked at me pityingly.

The discovery that there were different types of passenger on board this ship, people who got treated differently for reasons I could scarcely understand, was even more of a revelation to me than my first glimpse of the large steamer. I never really understood why we traveled to America First Class, a ticket my own grandfather could scarcely afford for himself. Maybe he believed that if Little Uncle and I were to start our new lives at the top, then luck would prevail and our lives would continue that way, as First Class passengers for life.

As the *Persia* sailed out into the ocean, our first evening aboard was punctuated by the sound of a gong booming throughout First Class. Little Uncle and I rushed into Uncle Poi Fun's cabin to find out what all the fuss was about. It was just dinnertime. We found him dressing for a formal dinner in white tie and tails. Fascinated, we sat on his bed and watched. We were particularly impressed with his silver cuff-links and pearl shirt studs. It seemed a tremendous amount of effort just to eat supper. Finally, with brilliantine applied to his hair as a finishing touch, he was ready.

"You follow me into the dining room and do exactly what I do with the knives and forks, boys," said Uncle Poi Fun. "We won't be eating with chopsticks, and you need to learn how to eat like a Westerner with silver cutlery and napkins. And remember, be very careful not to drop your plates on the floor. Please, please don't embarrass me."

Little Uncle and I had a lesson in the use of knives and forks before the ship sailed, and we had been measured for some Western clothes of our own in Hong Kong. We were wearing our new trousers and jackets as we walked in to dinner. I was amazed at the dining room; there was candlelight everywhere and the tables were filled with crystal glasses and shining cutlery. It was like a magician's cave filled with jewels and mysteries and strange folk. Sitting down, I picked up a fork and looked at it critically. I was not convinced that knives and forks were the best way to eat a meal and didn't believe that the starchy foreign clothes were an improvement on the ones I had been used to wearing. I felt terribly uncomfortable and out of place and the collar of my shirt bit into my neck and pinched the skin.

The dining room soon filled up with other First Class passengers. The gentlemen, like Uncle Poi Fun, were all dressed in formal dinner suits and the ladies in long dresses with shiny jewelry. Little Uncle and I appeared to be the only children in the entire dining room until I spotted a small Chinese boy standing in the corner of the room. He was charged with monotonously pulling a cord, which operated a rectangular fan that swung back and forth from the ceiling of the dining room. He looked friendly, and I waved to him. He tried to ignore me, then cautiously waved back. A steward spotted the boy waving and instantly smacked him on the back of the head by way of a reprimand. Some stern words were exchanged, then the steward glanced over at me, glared and shook his head. Little Uncle, who had seen the whole thing, laughed. My cheeks burned with embarrassment and I felt sorry for the boy who had just been smacked on my account.

As the courses arrived, Little Uncle and I sat at a table staring at the myriad of knives, forks and spoons in front of us. Little Uncle seemed to take to it all much easier than I. It seemed impossible to me that all of these things were necessary just to eat supper. Uncle Poi Fun, seeing my confusion, coughed and made us both watch him just to make sure we picked up the right piece of cutlery at the right time. The moon-shaped silver soup spoon was straightforward enough and that course went well, at least until I picked up the bowl to drink the last drops of the soup that I couldn't reach with the spoon. Uncle Poi Fun seemed to suddenly have a fit of coughing. As I stared over my bowl at him, worried he might be choking, Little Uncle giggled and kicked me under the table. Uncle Poi Fun made a stabbing motion with his finger, telling me to put the bowl down at once. He sighed. Sweat was forming on his forehead.

A waiter swung by and, moments later, the soup bowl had been whisked away and replaced with a plate, upon which sat a thin, flat fish, the likes of which I had never seen before. Uncle Poi Fun coughed again and we turned to him. He was holding a flat fish knife and a fork and trying to demonstrate how to slice into the fish, extricating all the bones in the process. It was then that I noticed the other passengers at our table watching this pantomime with a mixture of amused interest and irritation. One fat man was muttering something under his breath, something that sounded like "It shouldn't be allowed." He clearly disapproved of children of any kind being allowed in the dining room, or indeed in First Class. Trying to ignore his glaring, I nervously picked up the fish knife. Uncle Poi Fun coughed again loudly. He nodded at his left hand. I had the fork in my right hand and knife in my left. After I had swapped them around, Uncle Poi Fun sighed again and took a gulping drink from his wine glass.

With my special fork and knife at the ready, I looked down at the flattened fish on my plate. If this had been caught in the river at home and presented as food at the table, my grandmother would have had a few choice comments to make. I watched as Uncle Poi Fun sliced expertly into his fish. I gingerly attempted to follow suit and slide my knife into the flesh of the flat fish as my uncle had done. That's when my elbow caught the edge of the plate, flipping it upright, catapulting the fish into my chest and sending the plate crashing down onto the floor. The sound caused every head in the dining room to turn my way. I wanted to hide under the table.

Following this incident, it was decided that I should spend the rest of my journey to America banished to our cabin during mealtimes. I could eat my food there and make as much mess as I wanted. Uncle Poi Fun wanted to avoid any more scenes.

After a few days, the wonderment of being on board the steamer faded and I grew very homesick. I took to walking the decks of the ship alone during the day, and I found that if I sat on a First Class deck near one of the staircases that led to the lower decks I could hear the voices of my countrymen gaily talking below. The familiar Cantonese sounds were comforting in this alien world of foreigners, etiquette, strangely shaped fish and customs I didn't understand. I had been doing this for a few days when I heard a familiar accent spoken, the dialect of my home village. Leaning as far as I could over the rails, I saw a huddled group of Chinese people chatting and laughing together; amongst them was a familiar face, my village-mate Chang Wai Cheung. In later years he would rise to become a major player in the Chinese political system, but for now he was just another Chinese peasant traveling in Third Class to America. I was overjoyed to see a friend from my village. I shouted out, "Hey, Wai Cheung!"

He saw me and waved back.

"Who is down there with you?"

"Jung May and Quan Kin Sing. Come down here!"

"I can't. I am stuck up here in First Class with the Westerners. Uncle would be mad with me."

I pulled myself up onto the rail I was leaning on and swung my feet over. As I lowered them down on the other side of the railings, my toes found purchase on a small iron ledge. Keeping one hand on the rail, I leaned out over the void like an acrobat in a Chinese circus. I could see everyone clearly now and the smell of their food was making my stomach rumble.

"I'm hungry. Have you got any rice to eat?"

"They don't feed you in First Class?"

"Nothing you'd want to eat. Western food."

"Oh, sorry. We've got plenty of rice, and congee too."

I would have gladly given up traveling in First Class, and all of its fancy food and impossible cutlery, right there and then for a single bowl of my mother's chicken congee. She would carefully boil chicken pieces together with cupfuls of rice in a large pot of water for the longest time until the rice and the chicken broke down and became a thick, soupy porridge. It was delicious, especially when seasoning was added, and a staple of our diet back home. That's when I had an idea. Determined not to starve all the way to America or be confronted by another impossibly skinny fish, I engaged Wai Cheung's help. My plan was simple. I had befriended a cabin boy—from Canton, like me—who was willing to sneak the meal I was being served in First Class surreptitiously down to Third Class, where Wai Cheung would take it and barter with someone for a delicious meal of congee or chop-suey rice. I was in heaven when the familiar smells and tastes finally came up to my cabin. Suddenly a little bit of home was with me again.

3

ON THE ISLAND OF ANGELS

After twenty lonely days on board the SS *Persia*, passing through Manila and Honolulu, I finally arrived on San Francisco's famous and notorious Barbary Coast. It was October 1913, and the world before me was as alien as anything I could imagine. Later, when I was old enough to understand the misery and notoriety of those nine blocks of San Francisco with Pacific Avenue running through its dark heart, I came to wonder how many dreams of a better life and future had been lost and broken there. It seemed even stranger to me that a boy's first glimpse of a bright new world should be a shoreline where so many hearts had been broken by the looking-glass of narcotics and lost hope. San

Francisco's Barbary Coast was a way station of stories ending and beginning.

Beneath a dark Pacific-blue sky the ship's horns blared out, proudly announcing our arrival in the port. The deep booming summoned us up onto the top deck. As the skyline of San Francisco rose from the water, Little Uncle and I stood with Uncle Poi Fun watching the city's approach. A fine sea spray swept across the deck. I glanced down into the water below just as a shaft of sunlight caught the spray from the ship's bow, breaking it up into a shimmering rainbow of refracted colors. Moments later the rainbow was gone, the physics of pure light replaced by the swelling grey of the deep ocean water.

After packing up our belongings and boarding a United States government launch, we were shipped off to Angel Island. Every immigrant who wanted to start a new life in America had to go to Angel Island, a sort of concentration camp where they would be questioned and cross-examined by officials before being allowed entry into the United States. For a child brought up in a faraway land of temples and pagodas, this new world seemed to offer little that was familiar or comforting. Everything seemed so large and imposing to me.

In the years that followed, I would get to know the city, but I never lost my wonderment for it. Each tall building that towered above me, every steel bridge that spanned water to connect the land, the noise of motorcars and trams, it was all a revelation to me. I became fascinated with the engineering and science that created these marvels. The unforgiving steepness of the hills of San Francisco and throngs of people going about their business, all of them strangers in both custom and dress, were no less a surprise. Each new sight reminded me of the life and the world I had left behind and the people I missed there. There was no comfort for me now in memories, just cold newness.

This was also the place where I encountered open racism, hearing the word "chink" used for the first, though not the last, time. I remember encountering a sign outside a store that said, "No chinks or dogs allowed." It was hard for a nine-year-old to fathom that this slur was aimed at me. There seemed no rational explanation for it.

On the fifth day of my confinement on Angel Island, I was ushered into a small room for my interview. The immigration inspector was a kindly man and the interpreter was accommodating. Unlike other inspectors who I had heard used threats and abusive language to extort the truth or to justify their own suspicions and prejudices about immigrants, this team of two nice fellows did everything possible to make a nervous boy feel at ease and to help him along with the correct answers. They asked if I needed the translator; I did not. My grandmother had employed a tutor back in China to teach Little Uncle and me basic English in preparation for our journey. We both spoke the language.

"What is your surname?"

"Lee."

"What is your father's name?"

"Lee Sing Wai."

"And your mother's?"

"Sun Cheong Kiu."

"Are your parents living?"

"My mother is, but my papa is dead."

The inspector looked up. He smiled and patted me on the head.

"Who are your closest relatives?"

"Well, my Uncle Lee Tay, who has a farm in California, and I have Little Uncle who is with me on this island."

"Little Uncle?"

"My uncle! He's the same age as me."

"Oh."

"Almost."

"Oh. Have you any brothers and sisters?"

"No, sir."

"Can you tell me something about the house you live in, in your village at home in China?"

"It's a Chinese house."

"Yes, yes. Of course it is. Well done." The inspector smiled. "Now let me ask you one more question. What do you intend to do in America?"

I remembered what my mother had told me just before I left.

"I want to study hard, get a good job and make my mama the proudest mama in the world."

The inspector grinned and put the file away.

Two days later, Little Uncle and I were released to my grandfather's care by the immigration authorities. After taking the launch to San Francisco, we headed to the Tin Hop Company, Uncle Poi Fun's store on 732 Jackson Street, where we stayed for a month before heading up to my other uncle's farm outside of Walnut Grove, a small agricultural town built on the banks of the Sacramento River in Northern California.

Back then, the town spanned the east and west banks of the river, and a ferry was in constant use sailing back and forth between the two halves of the town. Walnut Grove was a town split in two, both physically and culturally. Whites lived on the west bank and Asians on the east. The eastern side of town was divided further into Japanese and Chinese areas. When a bridge was built in 1916, the ferry was consigned to town history. I missed the ferry and the part it played in keeping the townsfolk linked. I especially missed the sense of adventure I always felt the moment the vibrations began beneath my feet, telling me that its old engine was starting up.

My favorite time on the ferry was always when it rained. While other passengers took shelter, I would walk out into the middle of the deck and stand alone, partly protected from the elements by an old, weather-faded, black gentleman's umbrella of my uncle's. The umbrella was distinctive in that it bore the faded brass crest on its cracked cane handle of its makers in St. James's Street, London. How this umbrella came to Walnut Grove was a mystery, but I was glad of its faded elegance. Standing beneath it, I would watch the raindrops hit the river water, creating thousands of perfect little ballerina circles that expanded outwards around the ferry. I was living between two worlds, the China of my past and the America of my future, and like the ferry, I felt belonged to neither shore but somewhere in between.

As a small boy I had watched the same scene with my mother many times in Dai Waan. The sight of rain falling on river water was and is still magical to me because of her. "Watch the dancers skipping on the water, Ah Nom," she would say. "Can you hear the music they are dancing to? Not everyone can hear it, but it is there if you listen hard enough and your heart reaches for out it. It will always be there, Ah Nom, telling you that your mother will always love you."

Then my mother would pull me close and hum quietly, rocking me back and forth in her arms, and I would fall asleep imagining a great symphony of music playing across the Dai Waan river for the thousands of tiny raindrops to dance to. Watching the rainfall come down all around the ferry, I could still hear her voice telling me to listen to the music. I hoped she still stared out across the river at home when it rained and thought of me.

During my youth, Walnut Grove supported the largest Chinatown outside of San Francisco. This came as something of a surprise to me, to find in a small, rural American town men openly walking the streets with their hair braided in long queues and wearing Chinese traditional dress. The

Chinese had been attracted to Walnut Grove because it provided them with an opportunity to start businesses of their own unimpeded by the racism that kept them out of the white-dominated job market. It didn't matter how qualified, experienced or educated you were; in the American workplace at the turn of the twentieth century, the only jobs open to Chinese immigrants were menial. Back then, the *life, liberty and pursuit of happiness* highlighted in the American Declaration of Independence seemed to apply to Caucasian people only. For me, it was always poignant that John Locke, the English philosopher who is often cited as the inspiration for that famous phrase, was also a principal investor in the Royal Africa Company, a notorious company involved in the slave trade. Despite the high-minded ideas that appear in his published writing, damning both the aristocracy and slave ownership, it appears that the English philosopher could, as one of my liberally minded high-school teachers would later quip, "Locke the other way" when it suited him.

Before the First World War, agriculture was one of the few opportunities open to the Chinese if they wanted to build a new life for themselves with some security. Even though it was still against the law at that time for a Chinese person to own land, they circumvented this obstacle by leasing farms from landowners happy to let others take the economic risk, do the hard work and then share the rewards. The California Alien Land Law of 1913 limited the leasing of farmland to immigrants to three years, but some landowners were happy to find clever ways to renew the lease if the farm was in profit and making them money. This is exactly what my uncle had done. His farm cultivated pears in a large, well-laid-out orchard that seemed to stretch for miles. Even now, when I slice open a pear and smell the fragrance of its juice, I am immediately taken back in time to the sight of the pear trees that were cultivated so lovingly by my uncle and his family.

At the heart of the farm was a ranch house where the whole extended family, including my grandfather, lived. My grandfather conducted his business trading goods alongside my uncle, and the house was always a noisy hustle and bustle of business deals being done or discussed. My grandfather would sit at the end of a long wooden dining table, like the chairman of the board of some multinational company, offering sage advice to whoever needed it—along with rebukes when necessary—and maintaining a strict eye on the bookkeepers who looked after the family businesses. Despite the noise and the ever-present throngs of children careening around the house, not much escaped his attention. As we were the latest and most junior members of the family to arrive and take up residence in Walnut Grove, there were no spare bedrooms available in the main house for Little Uncle and me. So we were assigned the attic. I loved it. It was large, spacious and quiet, a place of our own. With a single candle lit at night in the small window above my makeshift mattress bed, it was the perfect place to think and dream.

4

WILBUR CHEONG'S MANIFESTO

By January 1914 I had been enrolled in a country school a short distance from my uncle's farm in Sacramento. It was a small school made of clapboard and a single classroom. Its students were the children of farm laborers and local tradesmen and there was one teacher for all. You would have children aged from five to fifteen in the same class and nobody was expected to go on to achieve great things academically. If you could read and write by the time you graduated, that was judged to be enough of a success. The future was mapped out for those who attended and the schooling matched those aspirations. I found the place dull, but I was happy to pass my time there daydreaming. During summer vacations, I earned a few dollars picking fruit, allowing me to buy a few luxuries, and in time I adjusted to life in this new world.

In the summer of 1916, when the world far away was at war, a stylish young man called Wilbur Cheong arrived on our farm to pick fruit. He was a few years older than we were and still in high school, yet he had a curious habit that stood him apart from the other boys: he liked to smoke a pipe. Despite our age difference, he took a shine to Little Uncle and me and we soon became friends. Cheong was very smart, and he was also a progressive. His view, which he would call the 'Cheong manifesto', was that education was the only solution to the racism and economic discrimination that Chinese immigrants had to face on a daily basis.

He told me the story of his grandfather, who had come to America in the 1860s and was employed as one of the thousands of Chinese workers to help build the western leg of the Transcontinental Railroad. Wilbur told us he was paid $28 per month to risk his life on behalf of the great American economic revolution. Railroad construction was a risky business, especially in the treacherous high mountain passes of the Sierras. Chinese workers would be lowered down steep cliff faces in wicker baskets dangling from long ropes. They would then hammer out holes into the mountainside and plant explosives. These charges would blast holes in the rock through which the deep tunnels had to be mined by hand. When the wind whipped up and the weather turned bad, this was potentially lethal work, and accidents occurred regularly.

Wilbur's grandfather realized that he was never going to get rich dangling from a cliff in an old wicker basket. It was as he put the explosives in the hole he had just hammered out in the granite rock face that he had a brilliant idea. Twenty-eight dollars a month didn't amount to much buying power as an individual, but multiply that amount by all the Chinese workers building the western leg of the railway and you had a considerable amount of money at your disposal every month. The Chinese outnumbered the Irish by nine to one on the railway, and if he could persuade his countrymen to pool their money he would have considerable financial leverage.

After he had finished his shift that day he called a meeting with his fellow Chinese laborers and made a suggestion. He wanted to organize them into a society that would negotiate employment terms on their behalf with the white bosses. This wasn't a trade union, it was a cooperative. The cooperative would receive the agreed monthly pay for its members and distribute it fairly among them. This would ensure that everyone was paid properly and on time through a trusted bookkeeper employed directly by the cooperative. The railway bosses were happy to do this, as it saved them the expenses associated with payroll management.

Once this was achieved, Wilbur's grandfather then planned to expand the cooperative society's commercial activities on behalf of its members. He looked at the "run rate" associated with each individual Chinese laborer employed on the railroad. What did it cost the company to employ that worker, to house and feed him in the increasingly remote areas as the railway construction moved eastwards? Cheong's grandfather had another money-saving idea for the railway bosses and went to them with it. He asked them if the cooperative society could take over the housing and feeding of all the Chinese workers engaged in building the western leg of the Transcontinental. He believed that he could feed and house the Chinese workers at a far cheaper rate than the railroad company could ever compete with. The bosses immediately agreed, and part of the deal he struck to take over the housing and feeding of the Chinese workers in his cooperative was to agree on an increase in pay to $31 per man per month. This was one dollar more than the Irish were being paid.

Cheong Senior then did deals with merchants who supplied camping equipment, tents, supplies and food to the workers. He bulk-bought rice, fish, seaweed, dried oysters, dried meats, fruit and other staples, which would be stored by the cooperative society and prepared by designated cooks. A simple management levy was deducted from the Chinese workers' monthly pay packets to achieve this, and everyone was happy.

Another of the aims of Wilbur's grandfather's cooperative society was to ensure that each worker saved the majority of his pay and didn't fritter it away. So many of the Irish workers would be left with nothing at the end of the month after gambling, bordello and drinking debts were paid. Many of the Irish were working to simply exist, with no thought of tomorrow. This wasn't the case with Cheong Senior's cooperative members. Under his guidance, each worker was encouraged to save up to $20 a month from his wages—money that could be banked, sent home or reinvested under Wilbur's grandfather's guidance. The money the cooperative saved from the bulk purchasing of goods and supplies was also reinvested on its members' behalf. Cheong's grandfather used the profits he made to buy into the companies supplying the railroad contractors with goods and services. He saw the railroad business as a good bet and he wanted to be in on its expansion. The success of Cheong's cooperative society was soon emulated by Chinese laborers everywhere and, as a direct result, the Chinese came to be regarded by the white bosses as hard-working, easy to manage and an efficient workforce. When the Transcontinental Railroad was finally completed on May 10, 1869, Wilbur Cheong's grandfather was one of the crew of Chinese and Irish laborers who laid the last ten miles of track at Promontory, Utah. Retiring from laboring after the completion of this great railroad, Cheong used the money he had personally saved and the contacts he had made to build a business supplying skilled Chinese laborers to municipal and private construction contracts across California. He was an American success story.

When I met Wilbur Cheong, his grandfather had been dead for over a decade, but the young man still held him in high esteem. Wilbur's father had taken over the family business, yet had lacked his own father's business guile, drive and entrepreneurial flair. The company quickly ran into trouble without the old man's steady hand and vision to guide it. Realizing he wasn't cut out to run a business, Cheong's father made the mistake of allowing a second cousin to run the business on his behalf. Unbeknownst to him, this cousin secretly planned to set up a rival business and set about stealing all the contacts and contracts from Cheong's company. Worse still, the cousin was systematically embezzling money from the company to fund his own greed and ambition. By the time Cheong's father discovered the deception it was too late. He was out of business and the family in penury. Shamed by what he saw as his personal failure and weighed down by the money he still owed many creditors, Cheong's father committed suicide by hanging himself from a bridge on his son's ninth birthday.

Wilbur Cheong was devastated by this loss, but not destroyed. The tragedy also inspired him to be more than a sad footnote to history. He was determined to be more like his grandfather than his father and to restore the family fortunes. His mantra was that the Chinese needed to study harder than anyone else and then work harder in business than anyone else, so that one day in the future they could buy America. If America was anything, he used to say, it was for sale. There would always be someone somewhere ready to make a deal.

The example he used most to illustrate the Cheong manifesto of social change was to compare America to a hotel or a restaurant that consistently refused the custom of a Chinese immigrant. He said that it was every Chinese immigrant's duty to work hard so that one fine day they could buy that hotel or restaurant that refused us business. He estimated this process to take about three generations.

"Try stopping the Chinese from eating at the top table if we own it," he would say. "If immigrants were the majority shareholders in America's top businesses, then we could mandate change with the power of the dollar, the only language this brave new world truly understands."

He also proposed that racism and idiocy should be met with manners, wit and style. Cheong was a believer in what a fine tailored suit from London could say about a gentleman. A gentleman and his wardrobe were, to Cheong's mind, two inextricably linked ideals. He thought that exquisite tailoring was a form of impenetrable armor, shielding the wearer from ignorance and stupidity. There was one thing that Cheong was deeply suspicious of and that was the ascot tie. While he understood its appeal, he said that it belonged to the wardrobes of charlatans, roués and scoundrels. Ascot wearers could be wonderful luncheon companions and raconteurs, yet were not to be trusted with unmarried sisters, your fine wine collection and certainly not your checkbook.

Cheong lectured us on all manner of subjects pertaining to contemporary society, political intrigues, romance and the finer points of English tailoring as we picked fruits that season. Even though he was only a few years older than Little Uncle and me, Cheong's knowledge of the world appeared deep and unbounded by the two obvious facts of his social and financial status. Standing on a ladder with a basket of ripe pears hanging from his shoulders, his old clothes sun-bleached and torn, Cheong proposed that style was an elective state of mind and not hereditary, that being a gentleman was a choice well within the grasp of all men, no matter their background or circumstance. He was quite the most extraordinary person we had ever met.

Later in life I would, for fun, cut out the faces of my fam-ily from photographs and glue them into images torn from fashion magazines, advertisements and movie posters. If care-fully done, the new images could look quite perfect and you would have to double-check to spot the new additions. Every time I completed such a collage I would grin and imagine what Wilbur Cheong would have had to say about it if he could see these family parodies of high-society living.

Aside from buying America and indulging his suspicion of the ascot tie, one of Cheong's smaller projects was to convince my grandfather that Little Uncle and I would benefit from going to school in the city. Cheong thought the local school we were attending too provincial; he said we needed a bigger educational canvas upon which our future could be sketched with the bold strokes needed to design a successful life in America. He spoke like that all the time, in grand statements of intent, and felt so passionately about our future education that he took it upon himself to lobby my grandfather on the subject. Cheong's persuasive manner and eager charm won the day: at the end of the fruit season that year, Little Uncle and I left for Sacramento and, with Wilbur Cheong's help, enrolled in the Lincoln Grammar School on Fourth and Q Streets.

Sacramento was over thirty miles away from Walnut Grove, and the new school meant that Little Uncle and I would be staying part-time with relatives. The new school was much larger than the one in Walnut Grove. The classes were organized into ages and a proper syllabus was followed. Most remarkable was the mixture of nationalities that attended the school. There seemed to be over twenty-five different countries represented, from China to Eastern Europe to Western Europe to Latin America, India and Africa. The school, as I recall, was painted yellow, and it was a bright place to be in every sense of the word. Academically it was forward-thinking and, owing to its diverse mix, set out to make us all proud to be Americans without being ashamed of being Chinese, Mexican or African. I flourished during my time there and did well as a student. Art, history and mathematics were strong subjects and I made many good friends.

If Lincoln Grammar School was a beacon of forward thinking, anti-Asian sentiment among the white population was never far away. This was particularly aimed at the influx of Japanese immigrants into the area, but the Chinese got caught up in the backlash against the Japanese. The Alien Land Act that impacted my uncle was primarily focused on stemming the tide of Japanese coming to America. In Sacramento,

Japantown was located between Second Street, Fifth Street, L and O Streets, and, despite our cultural differences and history, I made friends with many of the Japanese students at Lincoln. The irony of these early friendships was not lost on me years later when I found myself on the run with my family from the advancing Japanese troops. It was hard to equate these innocent childhood friendships with the Japanese Imperial Army I saw march into Canton intent on the slaughter and destruction of the Chinese people. I often wondered during the Second World War whether any of my school friends had returned to Japan to join the Imperial Army. I also wondered what would happen if my old classmates were to meet again under these circumstances. Would our past matter? Or would indoctrination supersede the simple human bonds of friendship we had forged?

One of the great wonders of Sacramento to me as a boy was the first skyscraper to be built downtown. If time allowed, after school my grandfather and I would wander over to Fourth and J Streets to watch the new California Fruit Exchange building being built. Its ten-story-high structure was a local landmark and I wondered what it would be like to work on its top floor when it was completed. The construction crews who built it, dangling precariously from its girders and scaffolds, were equally fascinating to me. They seemed fearless, like pirates from a Douglas Fairbanks movie leaping from rig to rope, and I often had my heart in my mouth as I watched them nimbly bound from girder to beam balancing building materials, tools and long scaffold poles. If they saw my grandfather and me watching them, they would wave down to us, and I would discreetly wave back, hoping not to distract them, praying they kept their footing. It was high drama, quite literally, on the corner of Fourth and J Streets.

There was one construction worker who stood out for me as the bravest of them all. He belonged in a circus, not a construction site. Every evening, just before the workers' shift ended for the day, he would climb up to the very highest point of the building, exposed to sheer drops on either side, carrying a twenty-foot-long steel scaffold pole. Few people took the time to look up as they hurried home from work past the construction site, but if they'd paused just one moment to gaze at the skyline they would have seen something amazing.

While his fellow workers were clocking off and thinking of beer and food, the unnamed man would stand on the highest point of the building, facing the sun. As it began to dip down towards the horizon, he would begin spinning the scaffold pole around and around in his hands like a baton twirler. It was a breathtaking display of balance and skill. When I asked my grandfather why the man risked falling to his death like this every evening after work, he laughed.

"Ah Nom, this man is not trying to die, he is risking all so he can live. At home he is probably a very ordinary man with a very ordinary life. But up there, standing at the top of the world, for that moment he is something more. He is challenging the sun to come and try and knock him from his perch. And every day it fails to do so is this man's personal triumph, his reason to live. He knows one day it will succeed and he will fall, but that day is not today. Today he is alive."

I didn't understand my grandfather's explanation at the time; it wasn't until I got older that I finally grasped what he was trying to tell me. Life is brief and death inevitable, and in the great swath of time all human achievement will be rendered to dust. But like that silhouetted man standing on the highest point of human endeavor he could find, we must be defiant in the face of these certainties. Should an opportunity to be brilliant arise, you must seize it with all your heart and passion, because you never know what eyes are watching you from afar.

Shortly after America entered the First World War, I came home from grammar school to find my grandfather sitting on a chair in my bedroom at the lodgings he had arranged for Little Uncle and me in Sacramento. He had been waiting for me all afternoon to return.

"Hello, Ah Nom," my grandfather said. "I have come to say goodbye."

"Goodbye?"

"I am going home, back to your grandmother. I promised her years ago that one day I would return and that we would see out our last days together."

"Grandpa?"

"I am sorry, Ah Nom. I had always planned to go back to China once you were settled. But I thought I would make a few more dollars first to help me by in my old age. It also gave me a little more time with you. I hope you choose to go to college and be somebody in this world someday. When I am gone, Uncle Tay will take care of your school expenses."

My grandfather left America shortly afterwards to retire in the village he grew up in, returning to my grandmother as he had promised her all those years before.

Another link to my past had been severed.

5

UC BERKELEY

By the winter of 1922, I had graduated from high school and enrolled in the Iowa State College of Agricultural and Mechanic Arts. I was anxious to see more of America than just California, and as Iowa accepted Chinese students, it seemed a perfect place. Iowa was as far removed from my life in Sacramento and Walnut Grove as anything I could imagine. Engineering was also the career my uncle had impressed upon me to follow since I had stepped off the boat—a career endorsed and encouraged by my grandfather through all those sightseeing trips to downtown Sacramento to watch the city's first skyscraper being built. He believed this was the future.

"Things always need to be built in America, bridges, factories, cars and machines of every kind," he would say, "and you, Ah Nom, should be the one to build them."

I decided upon engineering just to please my uncle and grandfather. They had done so much for me and it was the least I could do to repay their kindness. Staring out of the window on the train heading east, I felt a nagging concern at the back of my mind about the wisdom of this course. I understood that engineering was a solid profession; I just wasn't sure how suited I was for it. What had impressed me as I watched the skyscraper being built was the courage and skill of the workers. The poetry of their long shadows cast against the building's superstructure. They were real supermen to my mind, separated from mortals like me below by their courage, skill and endeavor—men who created monuments that would last for hundreds of years or more. I was not interested in the type of concrete or pilings used in the foundations, nor the type of air-ventilation systems employed or the load-bearing stress tests that would need to be done. I had two passions, art and mathematics. If I pursued art, the odds of success were stacked against me, not to mention the disappointment it would cause my uncle and grandfather. Mathematics was a safer bet, yet math couldn't be the whole story; plus, I thought, there would at least be some use for mathematical aptitude in engineering.

I arrived in Ames at two o'clock in the morning. It was freezing and the town was covered in a deep blanket of compacted snow. A biting wind whipped around every corner, cutting through even the thickest of coats and trousers. Standing on the station platform with the snow falling almost horizontally and my two suitcases at my feet, I did my best to ignore the cold and tried to get excited about Ames. This town was, after all, supposed to be the start of a new, bright future for me.

The next morning, after a chilly night's rest in a local hotel, I called a cab and headed to the college. As the cab drew onto campus, I saw that the place was a ghost town. Nearly all the students had deserted the college for the Christmas holidays. The feeling of anticlimax was palpable.

After a little wandering around I finally found a caretaker who pointed me in the right direction. I took up residence in a hall with some other Chinese students who had nowhere else to go, and together we waited the holidays out alone. It was a cold and depressing time for me, until the college finally sprung back into life after the holidays.

When classes resumed, I opted for the Foundry Practice elective—a course designed to test engineering aptitude—and soon found out that engineering hated me as much as I hated it. The realization of the big mistake I'd willingly made was worsened by the fact that Ames was a backwater town with few distractions for a young man. Even life on a fruit farm was more exciting than this place. By April of 1922, I could stand it no more, and I made a decision. There was a world out there I wanted to experience, and if it wasn't coming to Ames then I would go out to meet it head on. I decided to abandon Ames forever and go on a road trip. I would see Chicago, Minneapolis, St. Paul and South Dakota and then head back to California. I chose these places randomly on a map with a pin. I allowed myself five pins and, closing my eyes, let my hand hover over middle America. Looking back, it seems a strange thing to do, but I was young and wanted the gods of chance to rule my destiny.

Racism was everywhere and accepted as the norm, yet even though I was forced to sleep in the open some nights after hotels refused my money, I didn't care. I believed I was lucky to be alive and to have the opportunity to see so many wonders in so many cities. I was convinced that I was witnessing the birth of a great country as it entered the modern age, a country that my children and children's children would love and fight for because it had dared to become a haven of light for the oppressed, the lost and those without hope in a dark and troubled world. I held firm to the conviction that I was the face of this country's future, not the bigots who denied me entry to a diner to buy coffee on account of my skin color. It would not be long, I believed, before the stupidity of racial intolerance would be done away with forever. It is now 1955 and I am still waiting, yet I have not given up hope that a man will come whose singular voice and dreams of a better world for our children will change everything. Hatred, like a bush fire, ultimately consumes those who propagate it, leaving nothing but scorched, barren earth behind in their hearts. Love, the greatest of reckless endeavors, inspires men to greatness in the face of seemingly insurmountable odds. Even though over half of my life is done as I write these words, I still hope to be given the opportunity to embark on a great and reckless endeavor. Maybe this book is just that, a reckless endeavor of the heart. A book I do not expect to see published in my lifetime, but one that could speak to, comfort and inspire my children, grandchildren and their children in a time when my name is just a memory carved in a tablet of stone on a grassy hillside.

After my road trip I decided to give engineering one last try. I entered the summer school of the University of California at Berkeley to make up for the lost credits due to my transfer, then enrolled as a regular engineering student in the sophomore class in the August of that year.

As it was for many young men my age at university, the pursuit of girls was very much on my mind. I'd only managed two serious dates, hardly enough for Casanova status, when I was introduced to Bobbie. Her parents, who had come to America twenty years before from Canton, ran a store in San Francisco that imported goods from China. Cute and demure, she enthralled me instantly and we wrote to each other often. Bobbie's letters were long and inspiring, her writing beautiful and captivating. Widely read, she could quote from almost anything, yet she was tactful and diplomatic and realized this could be boorish. If you didn't know the author or the book she was quoting from, Bobbie would always treat it as a charming foible that made you even more endearing to her. Age and experience and the compromises of adulthood can encourage cynicism, yet the memory of my first love has stayed with me into later life and remained true. The first notes of a cello playing a certain concerto can sweep the curtains away from my mind, and I can see, as if through a window, the place and moment I first heard it with her. Age has changed me, but the memory of the young people we once were and that time we spent together remains part of me today. An inexperienced heart feels everything so keenly and those brief, brightly lit moments of first love with Bobbie were some of the keenest.

I was still studying engineering at UC Berkeley in January 1923 when I, along with another Chinese student, was offered a vacation job at an engineering company in Milwaukee, Wisconsin. Needing the money and thinking the experience might prove useful in the future, I took up the position and left the sunshine of California behind again. After the Ames experience I wasn't keen on the Midwest, but my classmate felt differently.

"You know, Steve, I am glad of the chance to get the hell out of California for a while."

"Really?"

"Well, for one thing, have you ever tried to use one of the barber shops on College Avenue or book a table at a decent restaurant in San Francisco? The moment they learn you are Chinese, it is 'no.'"

An image of Wilbur Cheong's smiling "I told you so" face flashed into my mind.

"And you think that the Midwest will be better?"

"Perhaps not, but it can't possibly be worse."

When we arrived a week later in Milwaukee, we met with the personnel director for a brief interview and then were put on the factory's payroll, starting out on the plant floor. Working there I got to know many of the firm's long-term employees, many of whom were Chinese like me. Nearly all of these workers had graduated with distinction from universities like MIT and Harvard, and now they were stuck doing menial jobs. Nobody would give these highly educated men a better job because of their race. That shop floor was more qualified than the bosses who ran the plant. And this was the great American dream I'd traveled thousands of miles from China for?

Disgusted, I quit the job and hopped on the first train back to sunny California. Inspired by Wilbur Cheong's words—change brought about by the power of the dollar—I decided to shift my major to economics. This change of heart wasn't easy for me. I had just spent the last two years studying to be an engineer, and if I was to graduate with the class of 1926 in economics, it would mean studying every minute I wasn't sleeping, eating, in the bath or shaving. It was tough, but I did it. Cheong would have been proud.

6

GRADUATION

I often idled away my free time at university playing musical instruments for whoever cared to listen. On occasion I would be asked to perform at a friend's birthday party, and I even earned money one night playing with a local band at a concert after their regular ukulele player came down with flu. My extended family had always been a musical one, and I grew up with instruments lying around the house. I found learning a new instrument relatively easy and could master most within a couple of months of practice. Whenever I struggled, there was always someone on hand who could show me the correct way to grip a fret and fingerboard or explain a technique relating to the embouchure of a particular wind instrument. Music meant that I was never bored as a child, and I carried my love of it and the handful of instruments I could play into young adulthood.

With my graduation from university fast approaching, I wrote to my Uncle Tay asking him to come to the Commencement Exercise on May 15 at the new stadium at Berkeley. I wanted him to be there on my big day, to see the fruition of the sacrifices he had made on my behalf. Sadly, he couldn't get away from the farm, but he sent his son Johnman and cousin Howard to represent the family. Standing surrounded by thousands of graduates, all wearing caps and gowns, listening to the speakers and the Varsity Band playing the popular songs of the day, I said a silent prayer of thanks to my mother, hoping that the cool breeze in the air above us could carry it across the oceans that lay between us.

After graduation, my immediate problem was to get a job. Writing hundreds of letters to potential employers, I hit a solid wall of rejection. With nothing else to do, I took advantage of this period of limbo and enrolled in postgraduate courses at UC Berkeley, hoping that a thorough grounding in the science of economics would make me more employable. Finally, my persistent letter writing paid off, and on November 19, 1926, the eve of the big game between Stanford and UC Berkeley, I received a letter from Mr. Kong Poy, the Chief Cashier of China Toggery in San Francisco, asking me for an interview. One interview later and I was employed as a bookkeeping clerk on $80 a month.

I worked at the China Toggery for four months. The job was steady, yet that nagging feeling came over me again that settling down to this, into the routine of a job and a sedentary life as a bookkeeper, wasn't really what I was meant to be doing. Racial abuse against the Chinese was widespread in the United States and the daily reminders that you were a second-class citizen, even if you happened to be a UC Berkeley graduate, were everywhere. True, the living was comfortable and the Chinese community large enough to buffer you from the abuses you were conditioned to accept as a part of your daily life. But this racism never sat well with me; I was ambitious. And employment at a major bank or other white-run American corporation was simply not an option for a Chinese graduate, no matter how good his grades or aptitude. I was the wrong race. Initially enthusiastic replies to job applications suddenly evaporated when the personnel department finally worked out that the Mr. Stephen Lee who had written to them was unlikely to be a distant relative of the general who had surrendered to Ulysses S. Grant at the Appomattox Court House. It was a tough lesson in how America really worked in those days, and I began to grow resentful of having the door slammed consistently in my face for no other reason than where I was born.

That's when the thought of returning to China to see my mother first entered my mind, one so strong that I simply had to act upon it. I had about $150 saved up, not a fortune, but a start. If I wasn't going to return to China rich, then

I thought that I'd at least return looking employable. So I invested in two business suits and purchased a tan leather-trimmed trunk for my other belongings. Looking back, it was a reckless decision, but the urge to see my mother again made all other considerations pale. If I didn't go now, I would end up married and settled in the United States and the chance to see her again would have passed by forever. Not even the fact that a war seemed inevitable between the Chinese Communist Party (CCP) under Mao Zedong and the Nationalist Kuomintang Party (KMT) under Chiang Kai-shek in China could turn me from my path. If anything, it made me more determined. My mother and grandparents were getting old and lived alone, surrounded by a retinue of aging servants. If China was going to descend into civil war, I had to make sure they were safe from harm.

Before I left, I had one very important thing to do. I traveled to Sacramento to see my uncle and tell him of my plans. As expected, Uncle was not entirely happy about my decision to leave America.

"You do realize that there will be civil war in China soon?"

"Yes."

"And that doesn't concern you?"

"Of course it does."

"Well, you are either very brave or very stupid," my uncle said. "You left China almost wearing a diaper, and now you're going back with little more in the way of possessions to your name. You know that you can't live on good intentions. Tell me, how do you expect to find a job? You need to know people to do that, especially in China."

"I plan to burn my US papers to motivate me to resolve that problem."

My uncle's face told me exactly what he thought of my youthful arrogance. I tried to reassure him that everything would work out for the best, but he wasn't convinced. Age and wisdom gave him a very different perspective on what I was doing. I wouldn't listen to reason or argument, though; my mind was made up.

On my return to San Francisco, I made good on my promise and burned my American visa and papers in a small ceremony of my own. Then on April Fool's Day of 1927, four short months before the Nanchang uprising and the start of ten years of civil war, I boarded the steamer *President Jefferson* and set sail for China.

7

THE RETURN HOME

The San Franciscan afternoon was filled with bright sunshine, not the usual grey fog, as we headed out of the bay and away into the Pacific. My cabin in steerage was utterly foul, filled with stale cigarette smoke and unpleasant odors, but I had no choice but to endure it. My First Class trip to the United States was now a distant memory; I was returning to China as a Third Class passenger and this was my new reality.

During my time in America I had learned to play the piano, cornet, saxophone, clarinet and banjo. Realizing that this trip to China could be a lonely and dull one, I had brought my banjo with me. I'd sit out on the Third Class deck each night and play it to anyone who cared to listen. This nightly activity got me out of my terrible cabin and helped me make a few acquaintances with whom I could pass the hours.

On one of these nights, I was playing a particularly sentimental song on the banjo when I noticed a girl standing opposite me in the shadows. Her face was obscured from view. As I finished playing, she stepped forward and I saw her face, sharply drawn by silvered moonlight, for the first time. The girl was in her early twenties, delicate, with porcelain skin and jet-black Louise Brooks hair. As we exchanged pleasantries, she told me that she had been living in Los Angeles and was now on her way back to Hong Kong. Compared to the girls I had met at college, she was extremely forward; in the parlance of the day she would have been called a flapper. When we discovered that we knew some people in common in Hong Kong, our friendship was sealed.

Each night after supper I would find her waiting for me to come up onto the Third Class deck with my banjo. She would sit quietly on an upturned crate and watch me as I played. She was only interested in music that struck a melancholy note, so I played all the popular songs I knew from Twenties' America, slowing their melodies right down, keeping the themes and hooks, but rendering them into mournful reflections of the tunes we all knew so well. These half-caught memories of the familiar gave the girl, I suppose, a looking-glass in which she could see glimpses of the people she had once held close and danced with. In the chords I played there hid a way to transport her back, albeit briefly, to another time and place. One that had been washed out by the noise and brilliant light of the present, yet had lain hidden there all the same, just a breath away, as potent as ever, waiting to be recalled from oblivion by a single note of a song. Our love affair was conducted like this: two people sitting on a Third Class deck with the booming throb of the ship's engines turning below, people's voices chattering on the promenade decks, and an endless canopy of starlight above. We barely spoke. I played my banjo and she sat, a silent, half-shadowed figure cast in moonlight, staring out across the ocean. Finally, after five nights of happy, shared silence, she spoke.

"I wish we could be on this boat forever."

I had learned early on in my life not to make too many attachments to people; they had a habit of leaving you or being taken away. What I wanted didn't really come into it. Keeping people at a discreet distance was a habit born of necessity and a hard habit to shake. She sensed my reticence.

"Will I see you again?"

I didn't reply. I simply leaned forward and kissed her on the forehead.

She sighed. She seemed to know what I was saying without words. She was lonely and brokenhearted and I wondered whether I was making the biggest mistake of my life.

On April 22, 1927, after twenty-one days steaming across the Pacific Ocean, I saw Shanghai for the first time. I had read about the city and had always wanted to see it for myself, so I had planned to disembark to explore the city, then take a boat to Hong Kong the following week. My ticket took me only this far.

The girl whom I had romanced with music all the way from America came to see me off the boat. Amid the shouts and arguments of coolies soliciting to carry passengers' luggage, and in full view of the entire Third Class deck, I gave her a long and passionate kiss. I didn't care what anybody thought. I can't remember how long we stood there, but eventually a steward tapped me on the shoulder, coughed and asked us to step aside so other passengers could get by. Stepping back from the girl, I smiled; I knew that the time had come to leave. I headed towards the gangplank with my suitcase and coat in hand. I was resolved. Then, about halfway down the gangplank, I stopped. Forcing my way through angry and protesting passengers, I ran back to her. My heart was beating so fast I could scarcely keep my hand from shaking as I wrote my address on the back of a matchbox. Handing it to the girl, I promised to write her as soon as I could. She held the matchbox carefully in the palm of her hand as she stood looking at me, not saying a word. I picked up my suitcase and walked away.

As I reached the dock and stepped from the gangplank, it was as though a spell had been broken. I glanced back up at the steamship and the Third Class deck I had just left. The girl still stood there, gazing at me silently, her face now lit by the sharp Shanghai sun, and I could see that she was crying. As I raised my arm to wave goodbye, a reflected and refracted beam of sunlight bounced from the silver clasp on her jacket, blinding me with a brilliant flash of light. As I blinked and my eyes readjusted themselves, I saw her walk, as though in a shimmering haze of color, towards the ship's railings, lean over and let the matchbox fall from her hand. As the matchbox tumbled down into the harbor water below, the girl turned and vanished into the throng of passengers. I never saw her again.

After a week staying at the Oriental Hotel in Shanghai and touring the city, I made plans for the final leg of my journey to Hong Kong. There were plenty of distractions for a young man that could have kept me in Shanghai forever, but knowing that my past and my immediate future lay in Canton, I booked a ticket on the *President Lincoln* bound for Hong Kong. Not wanting to endure Third Class again, I invested twenty US dollars, a huge sum for me at the time, in a First Class cabin. While comfort was a consideration, what was really driving me was the need to set myself up on arrival in Hong Kong. My uncle's comments about not knowing anyone who could give me a job were still ringing in my ears, and it didn't take much working out that the people I needed to meet were more likely to be in First Class than in steerage.

The *President Lincoln* set sail for Hong Kong from Shanghai on May 5, 1927. The trip was due to take two days but engine trouble delayed us for four, a stroke of luck as it gave me double the time to try and meet everyone I could in First Class.

Nothing could, however, have prepared me for the surprise of meeting Mr. Chang Wai Cheung one night at the bar. He was the very same Chang Wai Cheung who had bartered my First Class food for congee on that first trip to America. Now a First Class passenger in his own right, Cheung was also an aficionado of single-malt whisky, wine and Cuban cigars. His time in America had not been entirely wasted; he had seized every opportunity to experience what the Western world had to offer. It had changed him superficially, but he was wise enough to remember, and value, the village and the circumstances into which he was born.

My old friend was as pleased to see me as I him. Cheung was politically ambitious, with high-level links to the nationalist government, and could prove a useful ally in my search for employment. Few jobs were ever advertised in China; they tended to be filled by recommendation and close connections within the establishment, of which Cheung had many. It was a lucky meeting.

When the *President Lincoln* docked in Hong Kong my plan was to head straight to Canton, then the biggest city in South China. Luckily, Cheung, who also had business there, decided to come with me. When I revealed to him that I was down to my last few dollars and needed a job, he readily agreed to help. Once we had rested and freshened up at the Asia Hotel, he took me to meet a colleague of his, General Awyang Kul, who was at that time in charge of the Tiger Port Administration. Within the week I was offered employment as the general's new English-speaking chief of staff. My duties were to prioritize his correspondence, organize his office and schedule, represent him at meetings he couldn't attend, précis reports that came in and highlight the most urgent ones needing his attention.

My plan had been to write to my mother and grandparents the moment I had secured employment and somewhere pleasant to live, but Uncle Tay must have already written to them. Grandpa and Mother didn't care if I was living in a leaky tea crate filled with straw at a railway station, they were coming to see me and that was that. They made the long trip to Canton from my home village within the week, leaving behind my grandmother, who wasn't feeling well. When I saw them, they had both aged, but they were still the same people I loved.

"Grandpa, Mother," I shouted as the porter brought them into my modest digs.

"Ah Nom," Grandpa said, looking me up and down, noting how tall I had become and smiling as though this was the happiest day of his life.

"Let me take a look at you, Ah Nom," said my mother as she opened her arms and waved me to her. As I walked towards her, she began to cry. For a moment I felt as if I was that small child again, the one who had watched her image vanishing into the distance on that long-ago road; yet now that road had brought me back to her. I was home.

8

MY NORTH STAR

After Grandpa and Mother and I spent a few days together, they went back to the village, and on the first of June, 1927, I went to the Tiger Port Headquarters and reported for duty.

My mother wrote every week asking me to come back to the village to see her, but I declined. I needed to ensure that the job was secure, plus I had promised her I would build a house in Canton where we could live together as a family again, and I wanted to focus on earning the money for that. Three months had gone by when a telegram arrived from my grandparents in the village saying that my mother was very ill. Regretting my decision not to visit earlier, I asked permission to take time off from work and immediately headed there, expecting the worst. When I arrived, I found my mother hale and hearty, clearly not at death's door. That's when she confessed that she'd sent the telegram herself, that it was the only way she could get her son back to the village. It was hard to be angry.

The village had changed little since I had left, and apart from the odd civic improvement, the only major changes were to the faces of the people who lived there. Even though I was yet to make a success of my life, I realized for the first time that nobody here cared very much whether I was rich or not. They were simply happy to have a prodigal son return and to be reunited as a family. After a few days, when it was time to go back to my job in Canton, I promised my mother that she would not have to invent any more sudden illnesses to get me home again.

Back then China was a country ruled by endemic corruption and economic chaos. Popular resentment against the rich, ruling political elite was growing and the seeds were being sown for the Cultural Revolution. Power struggles occurred at all levels of Chiang Kai-shek's nationalist government as people jockeyed for positions of influence and power. Being employed in key government departments was a surefire way to line your pockets with bribes and facilitation fees from businesses and the public alike. Everyone accepted that in order to get anything done you had to pay a bribe to an official or several officials to expedite your plans. Early on in my working life I decided that I would neither pay bribes nor take them.

I had been working for General Awyang Kul for five months at $140 per month when a powerful political opponent ousted him from his job. The new guard wasted little time in having the general's entire roster of key lieutenants taken into custody on corruption charges. Even though I had only been in the job a short while, I decided that it was safer for me to head back to Hong Kong and seek work there until the miniature power struggle had passed. I didn't want to get caught up in the mess left by General Awyang Kul's departure. My trip to Hong Kong proved fruitless, though, and when my money ran out I was forced to head back to Canton. When I got back to my residence I found a money order for a thousand Hong Kong dollars waiting for me from Uncle Tay in America. How could he have known what I was going through? My mother writing to him was the only answer I could imagine.

Back in Canton I wrote to every prospective employer I could think of including, everyone I had met on the steamer to Hong Kong. Among the polite replies I received was one from Mr. Lum Man Chin, another First Class passenger I'd exchanged details with. He had just taken up an appointment as the new head of the Canton-Kowloon Railway and was looking for an English secretary. Thinking I had been rescued, I wrote back saying I would be honored to accept the situation. Unfortunately, the day before I was to join, a letter arrived from Mr. Lum with the news that the job had already been taken. He had fallen foul of a powerful political clique that wanted the job for one of its own.

It was a knock to my confidence. China was a contrary and difficult place, yet it was the world I had chosen to step back into and one I would have to learn how to navigate somehow without abandoning my principles. In America, I had faced discrimination on account of race; in China it was corruption and the ever-present precipice of economic chaos.

Then, in March 1928, my luck finally changed. My prolific letter writing paid off when a clerk who didn't require his palm being crossed with dollars passed my curriculum vitae to a very powerful man, General Cheung. The job in question was related to the handling of money, so I assumed that they'd wisely decided not to employ someone who had bribed his way into it. If the books didn't add up at the end of the year, it would be the bosses who would take the blame. Cheung ran the Aviation Bureau, a civil appointment, and I was appointed as its treasurer on $172 a month.

With a regular salary in place and the prospect of stability, I was happy to simply get on with life, but my mother had other ideas. She felt the time was right for me to think about marriage and starting a family of my own. While I understood what motivated her, I was reluctant. The world in which I was living felt very impermanent, and the idea of bringing children into it when my whole life was so uncertain was not one I relished. I was still in this frame of mind when, one bright autumn Sunday afternoon, I ran into Mr. Lum Gee

Sum at a bus stop. He was a colleague at the Aviation Bureau.

"Hey, where are you going, Chief?"

Having few friends in the city, I had nothing else to do on a Sunday but wander around its streets, stopping to eat at stalls and to listen to musicians who sometimes performed outside one of the few Catholic churches in the older parts of town. I shrugged; I had planned to visit a tearoom and then walk back home. Mr. Lum Gee Sum was persistent.

"I'm off to visit my charming niece. She is quite a beautiful girl and has a lovely disposition. Why don't you come along? I'm sure you'll like her."

Without anything better to do, I was persuaded to go with Mr. Lum to his cousin's house. His niece, though, was not there. She was holidaying in Hong Kong. So instead of meeting the beautiful girl with the pleasant disposition, I found myself under the scrutiny of a gaggle of aging aunts and other family members who clearly viewed me with the greatest of suspicion. I sat there for a full thirty minutes sipping tea while nobody spoke a single word. Finally, when I felt it polite to do so, I drained the last drops from my teacup, refused a refill, made my excuses and left, my face burning hot as I hurried away down the street hoping I would never see anyone in the Lum family again as long as I lived.

I had largely forgotten the incident when one week later I bumped into Mr. Lum again.

"Hey, Chief, come with me again to see my niece. I'm sure she is home now."

I hesitated. I didn't relish another grim silence filled with glaring aunts over tea. Then suddenly a voice inside my head started shouting. It told me to go.

"OK. OK," I heard myself say, as if it were someone else speaking. "I will go with you, but I tell you, it's going to be the last time."

The door to the Lum family home was in sight and there was a part of me that wanted to turn and run, but for some reason I felt compelled to walk on. Upon entering the home I was shown into a sitting room. On the far side of the room, with her legs neatly crossed and her hands delicately placed in her lap, a striking young lady was sitting on a sofa and chatting with other members of the family. Before I had a chance to introduce myself, the girl's father walked up to me, grumbling something under his breath and shaking his head. He was clearly used to suitors appearing at the house and would prefer them all shot before they crossed the threshold.

"Mr. Lee, ah, yes, that is my daughter, Belle. I can see you would like a formal introduction."

He walked me over with the gait of a man being led to his execution. Belle already seemed to know who I was, judging by the pitying half-smile on her face. I was sure she was trying not to laugh. The story of my failed attempt to meet her had clearly been an item of much merriment at the Lum family dinner table that week.

"How are you, Mr. Lee. Won't you sit down?"

During the introduction, the entire Lum family sat silent

listening to every word exchanged, but they faded into the far distance for me. There are plenty of songs about love at first sight, and to someone who has never experienced that kind of immediate love they no doubt sound fanciful and ridiculous, but that is exactly what happened to me. I fell for Belle the moment she first looked at me and gave me that knowing, yet gentle, half-smile. I knew that she was the one, the girl I would spend the rest of my life with. Whether Belle felt the same way, I didn't know. Being a woman, and therefore far more sensible than I, she kept her heart to herself. I, on the other hand, turned into a train wreck of incoherent thoughts and half-conceived sentences that seemed to spill out of my mouth.

"Mr. Lum, my cousin, told me that you are from America."

"Yes, I came back last year."

"I like American returned students. They always seem like nice people. Don't you think so?"

"I don't know. I never thought of myself as someone who wanted to be described as nice. Nice people, to my mind anyway, tend to be a bit … you know. Oh, but that's not to say I'm bad."

"Really, you aren't nice?"

"No, no. I mean. Well, you know. When anyone says someone is terribly nice, I automatically have this image of the person they are referring to as someone a bit, you know, dull. In need of a good kick up the … you know what I mean?"

"I'm not sure I do, Mr. Lee? You want to go around kicking

nice people? Several of my aunts are very nice. Do you want to start with them?"

Belle pointed at the row of aunts, who were now actively glaring at me.

"Um, well. Perhaps ..."

Belle laughed.

"I'd stop talking if I were you, Mr. Lee. Just smile and pretend you've said something polite and uncontroversial about the weather."

Belle smiled over at her aunts, who all smiled back at her, then fixed me with an x-ray glare.

"Mr. Lee, my brother, C.Y., came back from America two years ago. He's a little older than you. Do you happen to know him?"

"Yes, C.Y. Yes, he's very nice," I said and gulped, realizing the mistake I made.

"He knows C.Y. and thinks he's nice too," Belle said to her aunts. They all shook their heads.

By now I was too scared to say anything else. Ignoring my dilemma, Belle made polite conversation for both of us. All I could do was sit there and utter monosyllables. I had to do something. I leaned forward and was about to whisper something to Belle when I noticed that the whole room of relatives had followed suit. They were sitting on the edges of their seats, leaning forward and determined to hear everything I had to say, whisper or not.

Bo King, on the far left, and the Lum family in 1923

"Will you, I mean, can you leave here, Miss Lum?" I mumbled, glancing furtively at the staring relatives. "Go out to have tea with me now?"

"But we're having tea here," Belle laughed, pointing at her cup. "I'm sure it tastes the same and it's also free."

A very wrinkled old aunt couldn't contain herself anymore; she laughed and spat an ivory denture onto the floor. Without a moment's thought, I scooped the teeth up with a handkerchief and handed them back to the old lady, who promptly dipped them in her cup of tea and popped them straight back into her mouth. She smiled and the whole room burst out laughing. I used the laughter to lean closer to Belle and whisper some more.

"No, it's not that. You see, I'm a stranger in China. What I'd like you to do is to show me around a bit, if you have the time and the inclination."

She smiled, understanding.

"All right, then, if you insist. Please wait just a few minutes while I put my coat on. You can talk to my aunts while I am gone."

I looked around the room. Everyone was smiling at me. I had passed a test of sorts.

Outside the Lum family home, and later in the teahouse together, my courage returned and I found myself able to make conversation. Halfway through our talk I found my hand touching Belle's. She made no attempt to move it. Our life together began with that—the simple touch of our fingers across a table in a teahouse.

Four weeks later I called upon Belle and took her out for dinner. Afterwards we went for a walk in the park. It was a crisp and cool late evening and the sky was cloudless. Finding a marble bench, we sat down and I offered her my coat. We sat, neither of us speaking, both of us gazing up at the stars high above in silence, listening only to the noises of a nighttime city in the distance: dogs barking, motorcar engines, the musical clatter of a broken bottle hitting a sidewalk, voices momentarily raised, then silent. Throughout my life I've tried to take note of when these moments happen. Moments when I try to remember exactly where I was and assign every single heartbeat to memory. I have always believed that at the end of your life it is these moments that you take with you—an imprinted sense of things that, when you close your eyes, will see you through that final opening door and guide you safely to that unknown landscape beyond. These moments are your North Star, the magnetic compass bearing of a heart that always leads those who listen home. My children, be keenly aware of these moments when they arise. They last for only seconds, yet they become, in time, the sea-smoothed beach pebble of shining glass that, when thrown, can bring down even the tallest and strongest of walls that a man can build around his heart.

"Will you marry me, Belle?"

"Do you think you love me enough to marry me? Do you really love me enough? Will you be able to love me enough for an entire lifetime?"

Without any hesitation, I put my arms around her waist and kissed her.

The answer was yes. It always was. It always will be. Even now, at some time in the future, one where I stand at your shoulder, always just out of sight but never far away, even then, my children, Amy, Huey, Rudy and Yvonne, be sure of these words. I will always love your mother.

Lum Bo King (*left*) with Sook Ying Leong, 1925

The author: Stephen Jin-Nom Lee, 1926

Stephen Lee and Lum Bo King ('Belle'), 1927

Postcard of SS *President Wilson*, on the 1955 sailing to the USA

Stephen's passport photo, taken
for his return to the USA

The family together in California,1959

Echo Lake, California, 1960. From left: May, Yvonne, Belle, Stephen, Rudy

Family gathering in 1960

Belle and Stephen with May Lee, *c.*1960

Stephen and the bride – the wedding of Huey and May, 1961

Belle's birthday, 1962

Stephen with grandchildren, 1968

Stephen and Belle, 1969

9

COLONEL STEPHEN LEE

As a newly married man, I had to focus on creating financial security and buying a home for Belle. Luckily, soon after our marriage, I was promoted from the treasurer's job to the head of the controller's department, which meant more money. The new job started on January 15, 1929, but was by no means safe. Two other people had occupied that same chair over the last twelve months, and both had been ousted from it. General Chang, who was in charge of the organization, had an openly hostile attitude towards college graduates and blocked their promotion. It was only when there was literally no other alternative that I got the job. All key positions in China in those days were essentially political in nature and the only way of ensuring a long tenure was to solicit the support of powerful political allies.

During the month of September 1929, Marshal Chiang Kai-shek appointed General Chang to head up the Ministry of Aviation for the Central Government in Nanking, the capital of nationalist China at the time. Chang's appointment was in recognition of his being the first aviator to make a successful long-distance flight across China. General Chang's replacement was Colonel Wong Kwong Yui, also known as Fred Wong. The new man's temperament couldn't have been more different. Curt and determined, Colonel Wong had a sharp mind that saw issues cleanly and plainly, without sentiment. He wasn't someone who would simply let things ride for the sake of expedience. He was modern in his outlook and thought that the old Chinese custom of resigning en masse when a boss was fired was quaint and, frankly, ridiculous. He was all about doing a good job and getting results, which earned the respect of everyone who knew him.

China was still largely under the control of Marshal Chiang Kai-shek, yet the rising Communist Party under Mao had begun to make headway through a powerful and effective grassroots propaganda campaign. The Nationalist government was under threat from both Mao and the powerful Northern warlords with their well-armed militias. There were regular outbursts of fighting, and the people of Canton suffered. War profiteers were quick to take advantage of the upheaval by hiking up the prices of everything. Simple things like food,

The author while serving in the Canton Air Force, 1928

clothing and lodging were being pushed beyond the reach of ordinary citizens. The central government's spending was far in excess of the revenue it could raise through taxes, with so many people unemployed. As the nation lost confidence in its own government, the value of bank notes and government bonds also depreciated. People watched their hard-earned savings evaporate while an elite few grew extraordinarily wealthy. This lack of confidence in the markets and the banking system in China made it almost impossible to conduct business, and the economy was in danger of grinding to a complete standstill. China's banking system was built on bales of straw, ready for a spark from a tinderbox of financial reality to burn it all down.

Back home we were preparing for a smaller upheaval of our own. At 11:30 p.m. on January 9, 1930, Belle and I welcomed our first child into this fractured and challenging world we had chosen to live in. We named her Amy, and from the moment I first saw her, my single goal in the world was to protect her, to make her as proud of me as a father as I was to have such a beautiful baby daughter.

With Amy's birth I now had a reason to work even harder. There would be bigger bills to pay and I needed to earn more. So in February 1930 I took on a second job, teaching accountancy in my spare time to students at Canton College, a private institution. The extra income was welcome, but it still wasn't enough. Though I wanted desperately to buy a home, we simply did not have enough money in the bank. There were plenty of ways to make money illegitimately, but I wasn't prepared to do that. If I earned money, it needed to be done honestly. That's not to say that I wasn't ever tempted to take the easy course. But every time the opportunity to accept a bribe came up, I declined. Something inside me simply didn't want to be like all the others.

Then, one bright afternoon, Colonel Wong summoned me to his office. He, like others in his position, had grown rich during his tenure; he knew how to work the system.

"Ah Nom, I have received a complaint about you."

"Sir?"

"Yes, from a contractor. You refused to endorse an accommodation fee?"

"Yes, sir. It is something I won't do."

"If I asked you to pay a bribe or to take one on my behalf, and your job and the money to feed your children depended on it, would you do it?"

"No, sir."

"Not even if it displeased me greatly?"

"I would not, sir."

"And is it true that you have taken a second job, Ah Nom?"

"Yes, sir."

The colonel smiled. He picked up a framed photograph from his desk and handed it to me. "My family."

"Sir?"

"So you won't take a bribe or endorse one under any circumstances?"

I handed the photograph frame back to Wong. "I have already answered that, sir."

"Good. You are trying to save to buy a house, aren't you, Ah Nom?"

"Yes, sir."

"You are a father, like me, and a father needs a home for his family. How would you like to build one in Tungshan? We're doing some urban planning there, as you know. Putting up houses for people who need them, like you," said Wong.

"A house, for me?"

How much money have you got saved up?" the colonel asked curtly. "Well, how much?"

"About eight thousand dollars."

"All right, go ahead, commission an architect and builder. I will take care of you and make up the shortfall. But I have one request of you!"

"Sir?"

"I want you to continue to be an honest man. I value trust above all things. Especially where my own business interests are concerned."

And that was that. The colonel's gaze shifted down to some papers on his desk. I stood there in front of the desk, not sure how to respond to his generosity. I was still thinking of something to say in gratitude when Wong looked back up.

"You still here? I hope you are not going to ask me to paint this house of yours as well?"

He sat back in his chair, looking at me with a serious expression. Then he smiled. "I imagine that this is news that you would like to share with your wife?"

"Yes, yes. Thank you, sir."

I kept the secret from Belle until the next morning during breakfast.

"You know something, Belle? I had a beautiful dream last night. I dreamt about a lovely house with a large garden full of flowers and you were sitting with Amy at your knee in a beautiful drawing room."

"What are you talking about?"

"I'm going to build a house for you."

"With what?" asked Belle, thinking that her husband was out of his mind. Then I told her what had happened.

The house was designed and under construction with the International Engineering Company in under a month. It was completed by April 1931, one month after my application to the Ministry of Commerce and Industry for a professional accountant's certificate was approved. I was now a licensed Chartered Accountant, allowed to operate in China. Inspired by my new home and professional qualification, I began to write articles on accountancy practice and issues, many of which were published in various professional journals, including the *Journal of Accountancy* in America. I was proud to see my name in print, and being published also served to raise my profile at home, in China. My salary was now $290 a month, allowing us to start putting some money each month into savings. I was able to buy Belle a few luxuries and employ a maid and nanny to help with the house and family; life was becoming more comfortable. We had a home and my career was taking off. Then, just as I began to feel confident about the future, another civil war erupted.

The tension between the supporters of Chiang Kai-shek and the opposition, largely the Cantonese from the south of the country, had resulted in the imprisonment of the Chairman of the legislative council, the Honorable Mr. Hu Hon Man—an act of hostility that sent all the Nationalist executives of Cantonese origin south, fearing that they might also be detained. They wasted no time in forming a new national government in Canton. General Chang Wai Cheung, the national air executive, and all his Cantonese fliers supported them by immediately coming south. As a result, the Canton Air Force was reorganized and enlarged in preparation for the conflict with Chiang Kai-shek and his followers. In June 1931, General Chang Wai Cheung was made commander-in-chief of the new Canton Air Force with Wong, now promoted to general, as second in command. I was given the rank of a full colonel and put in charge of purchase and supply.

The tension between Chiang Kai-shek and the Cantonese breakaway faction was cut short by Japan's invasion of the northeastern provinces of China on September 18, 1931. With a foreign invader in Manchuria, there was a rallying call for everyone to put aside their differences and to make a united stand against the Japanese. Internal conflicts could be settled later. As the coalition of Chinese forces was being rallied, the Japanese moved on Shanghai and forced China to accept their infamous 'Five Demands'. Despite the fact that the Chinese authorities accepted these terms, the Japanese, in an act of cavalier ruthlessness, began to bomb Shanghai on the evening of January 28, 1932. All Western powers with garrison forces located in Shanghai telegraphed their home governments immediately, requesting reinforcements to be sent to Shanghai to protect their nationals. Despite a flurry of formal diplomatic protests by the Western countries, the Japanese continued their aggression.

The Japanese invasion meant that factional differences were temporarily forgotten. Troops were sent to Shanghai from all

The author (*left*) with friend Sam Kong, 1929

over the country to defend China. Every province was asked to train more troops, and the Canton Air force dispatched the Second Squadron, commanded by Colonel Ding Kee Chu, to Shanghai to support the country's defense.

In March 1932, a peace movement was initiated and a ceasefire was proposed. China had no alternative but to agree to all of the terms, no matter how onerous. The country was simply helpless in the face of such a well-organized and powerful enemy. In due course, both sides ended hostilities. On May 5, 1932, a deal was signed. Despite the signatures on paper, though, China was never truly at peace from this moment on. The ink was barely dry on the peace accord when the factional power struggle erupted again within China.

General Chang Wai Cheung had been attending the Nationalist Party's conference in Nanking at the beginning of May 1932 when Marshal Chan Chai Tong, the military dictator in Canton at the time, issued an order for General Wong Kwong Yui to take over the Air Force Administration. As a result, nearly all of the current personnel of the Air Force under General Chang's administration were either reshuffled or dismissed. I was one of the lucky few to remain in my post. Soon after, General Wong asked me to serve under him as his personal English secretary.

I was at my desk on July 17, 1932, when news reached me that Grandpa had suffered a heart attack. I traveled home immediately and brought him to Canton, where I placed him under the care of Dr. Y. T. Chan. Within the week, the feisty seventy-five-year-old began to feel better and started pestering my grandmother and me to let him out of bed. He claimed he was feeling fine and didn't want to spend his entire time in the city being nursed by my grandmother when there was so much to do and see. The doctor finally relented and gave permission as long as Grandpa promised not to overdo it. It was good to spend time with both of them again, and I used the opportunity to thank my grandfather for all he had done for me. One way was to ensure that not a day passed in the city without my grandmother and grandfather trying out the lunch and dinner menus at the best restaurants in town.

They had been with me for about a month when my grandfather suddenly announced that he felt it was time for them both to go back to the village. I had become used to having him around again, and I was going to miss him. As he left, he told me to look after Belle and his great-granddaughter, Amy. He put his hand on my shoulder, squeezed it lightly and promised me that I would see him again soon.

"Ah Nom. You are a good boy and have grown up to be a good man. These last four weeks have been the happiest time in my life. Thank you."

They were the last words he ever spoke to me. Seven days later I received a cable with the news of his death. For days, I refused to believe that a man like my grandpa could have died. I had missed out on having a father, and my grandfather was everything to me. A world without the Old Man in it seemed impossible.

More tragedy was to follow. Soon after Grandpa died, my wife gave birth to a little girl. We didn't have time to name her; she had been born prematurely and slipped away from us after only a few breaths in this world. The death of our baby daughter hit Belle especially hard, and I did all I could to support and comfort her. I tried to remain strong, though inside I was in turmoil; I too was devastated by the loss.

There was worse to come. On August 6, 1932, at 7:10 a.m., Belle gave birth to a brave little boy. I named him Donald, and I loved him from the first moment I saw him. Donald was also premature, and as a result his condition was very delicate. We hired a special nurse to care for him, believing that if he could just grow stronger he would make it. Donald was determined to live with us for as long as he could, yet the struggle eventually proved too much. Our little boy died in Canton Hospital on April 5, 1933, at one o'clock in the afternoon exactly. The time is carved into my memory and I can still, after all of these years, feel the burning pain in my chest at the thought of our little boy's loss. My eyes have tears in them as I write these words and remember my two babies. Every beat of my heart carries with it an echo of aching sorrow for the little ones I lost. I only met them for the briefest of moments, but that doesn't matter. I was, and will always be, their father. I loved them all those decades ago and I love them still with each word I write.

After the tragedy of Donald being taken from us, Belle and I waited until we both felt ready to try again. Two years later, on May 30, 1935, at 2 p.m., Belle gave birth to an eight-pound baby boy. My father-in-law christened my son Kin Pak, and I gave him an English name, Hugh. In time my family would all come to call him Huey. It was normal practice for Chinese families to give their children both English and Chinese names at that time. Parents felt that an English name as well as a Chinese name gave their offspring the best possible chance of success in the future.

I had still not recovered from the loss of Donald and my baby girl, and I was an anxious and overprotective father as far as Huey was concerned. I would find myself standing over his cot each night simply staring down at him, a part of me still overwhelmed by the pink squalling miracle. I would stand there, believing that if I closed my eyes for a second, baby Huey might just vanish into thin air. This habit was something Amy noticed one evening.

"Daddy, why do you look at him so much? Huey's just a baby. He doesn't do anything but baby stuff."

I had always suspected that Amy worried that I loved Huey more because he was a boy, but it was never so. She was only five years old. Those hints of her feelings were there from the very beginning, but it was only as Amy got older that I realized it. By then I didn't know how to tell her that she was wrong. All of my children have, to one degree or another, been an endless, gentle conflict for me, a soft mystery I could never solve. The years we spent together as a family were studded with electric moments of fulfillment, yet there were times when we reached for each other and touched only the cold nothingness of disappointment, misunderstanding and tears. Amy grew up believing that I loved her less. If only she knew the truth. I remember the first full day without Amy around. She had gone to spend the night with a friend, Lucy, who lived just ten blocks away, but she might as well have been in London. At dinner I sat at the table staring at Amy's vacant seat. Even Belle was silent. Before going to bed, the absence of Amy's hug and kiss on my cheek, the absence of her light steps going up the stairs, made our home a tomb. That first night without my daughter was a brief glimpse of what my future would be like without my children around me. I hope she reads these words one day and forgives me.

10

INTERMEZZO

In the wider world outside the day-to-day dramas of my small but expanding family, Chinese politics were moving at a swift and spectacular pace. It was hard to keep track of the constantly shifting political backdrop against which we lived our lives. The economy was in freefall; there was no law to govern the issue of notes in circulation. Mediums of legitimate exchange now included silver coins, central bank notes, provincial bank notes, Hong Kong bank notes and United States greenbacks. It was under these complicated conditions that a new monetary policy was inaugurated by the central government on November 4, 1935. It was an attempt to stabilize the economy, but the truth was that the economy, like the political system, was beyond control. The measures would ultimately prove wholly inadequate to cope with the changes about to hit.

Civil war flared up again and on July 17, 1936, the Canton Air Force deserted en masse to Nanking. It was all started by a rumor that Chan Wai Chow, brother of Chan Chai Tong, had secretly changed his position during the negotiations between Chan Chai Tong and Chiang Kai-shek. It was suggested that he had hired a group of Japanese aviators to take over the Canton Air Force the minute hostilities ended. True or false, the thought of Japanese aviators running the Canton Air Force enraged our aviators. While no Cantonese, if given a realistic alternative, would have wanted to align themselves with a Nationalist government as long as Chiang Kai-shek was in power, the rumor was forceful enough to drive the Canton Air Force into Chiang Kai-shek's fold. It was seen as the lesser of two evils. I remember that on the morning of the coup, General Chan Chai Tong, realizing it was over for him, asked for asylum in the British Consulate in Sha-meen. I supported the desertion, yet it was sad to see him cornered like this. Despite his fall from grace, General Chan Chai Tong's tenure in office hadn't been a total disaster. Even though his plans for industrialization were never fully realized, he had helped to raise the standard of living for many people. He championed the building of factories and helped create jobs where there were none before.

After he had been driven from office, the Nationalist government took over the running of the Canton Air Force. With Chiang Kai-shek now in charge, I felt that it was time for me to leave the Air Force, and I resigned. Using a letter of recommendation from General Wong, who had left for Nanking with all the remaining pilots and air crew, I secured a position at the Canton Trust Company, a bank, as an assistant general manager. I welcomed this new post because on November 23, 1936, at 7 a.m., Belle and I welcomed another boy into our family, a healthy nine-pound baby we named Rudy. This new addition to the family would grow up to be cheerful, easygoing and happily lost in the stardust world of his private laughter. We were now a family of five.

Sino–Japanese relations were a common topic of conversation in the teahouses near where I worked. Most people felt that it was only a matter of time before the Japanese made another play for China, its population and resources. These rumors came true on July 7, 1937, a day that the Chinese people will never forget. The first shot was fired in Lo-Kau-Chio on the pretext of a missing Japanese soldier near Peking's Lo-Kau-Chio bridge. The rise of the Nazi party in Germany and the policy of appeasement had given the Japanese the confidence to begin empire building again. They calculated that the Western countries would be too concerned with the nearby threat to consider interfering in something happening thousands of miles away. Soon after the Lo-Kau-Chio incident, the Japanese attacked in full force and struck Canton and other coastal ports with air raids. As the evacuation order went out, most people sent their families away from the fighting, either to villages in the countryside or to Hong Kong and Macau. Fortunately, Belle and the children were already in Hong Kong for their summer vacation when the Japanese struck and they were out of any immediate danger. The British colony was, I felt, a safe haven for the family while I remained in Canton.

The enemy air raids intensified as the days and weeks passed. When Belle called long distance from Hong Kong to check that I was safe and eating properly, we would find our conversations interrupted by the sound of bombs devastating the city. It must have been frightening for her to hear the explosions. She was scared for me, but I always told her not to worry, that the district we lived in had no strategic importance and that I would be fine. After the call was over I would replace the receiver on its stand, turn off every light in the room, place an armchair in front of the big French windows that led out onto a small balcony, turn on a gramophone and sit down with a glass of Irish whiskey. I remember listening to the Intermezzo from *Cavalleria Rusticana* by Mascagni on the gramophone as I sat drinking, feeling the whiskey burn my throat and watching the dark, murderous opera of man-made dragon fire consume Canton. I had never felt so lonely in my life.

Despite the danger, I had no option but to stay and earn the money I needed to support my family. When I could afford it, I would commute to Hong Kong to see Belle and the children on weekends. On August 26, 1938, at around 4 p.m., I was behind my desk at the Canton Trust Company when the phone rang.

"Wei. Lee speaking."

"Mr. Lee, this is Mrs. Mary Ho speaking. Your wife gave birth to a girl. Both mother and child are doing fine."

Yvonne, our fourth child, had joined the family.

"I won't speak for long on account of the cost, but I wanted to congratulate you."

"Thank you."

The phone went dead.

I sat back in my chair and looked at my hands. Hands that now had the responsibility of caring for four children. I smiled. After a few minutes of reflection, I picked up some correspondence that required my attention, trying to refocus on the work at hand. As I began reading, the sound of an air-raid siren screamed into life, warning of enemy planes overhead.

Japanese military operations were intensifying as the well-organized and well-equipped Imperial Army made inroads against the Chinese troops sent to stop its advance. Despite gallant efforts, the Chinese soldiers were no match for the mechanized onslaught that had long been prepared. The organized resistance against the Japanese attack disintegrated and panic began to spread. Rumors of an imminent enemy landing in Canton sent waves of terror through the city. With the Chinese army close to collapse, the civil authorities gave the order for businesses, banks and factory owners to evacuate staff and all vital equipment from the city. The public was ordered to evacuate as well. The Japanese were coming.

On October 14, 1938, with the enemy closing in, I served notice to my staff at the Canton Trust Company. They were to leave the city immediately, take all important documents, account books and title deeds to Hong Kong and wait there for further instruction. I ensured that we had reservations on a government-commandeered tow-boat to ferry our staff and friends to safety. Then, in a hurried trip back to our house in Tungshan, I packed up a few essential belongings and left, abandoning the motorcar I had recently bought and all the rest of my worldly possessions in the process. I would not see our home again until after the war.

The boat took us to Shek-Ki. From there we took a bus to Macau and then a steamer to Hong Kong. Nobody spoke much on the ship; we were under constant threat of attack from enemy planes throughout the sea voyage. If we were sunk, we knew we could not survive in the shark-filled waters. We had all heard stories of packed passenger boats filled with women and children failing to reach their destination. One can only imagine the horror of what those families faced during their last hours: floating far out to sea with their children clutching at them for protection. With no hope of rescue, the only choice left to them as parents was when and how their loved ones, those they had failed to protect, would die. I felt lucky: if our boat sank it would mean only my death. My family was already safe in Hong Kong.

When we arrived, the relief aboard ship was palpable. I found my wife and children waiting for me at the accommodation I had rented for them some months before, and we tried to pick up what we could of normal family life. As long as the Canton Trust was superficially still functioning, I had an income and a job. Meanwhile, the Japanese gains in China grew more extensive and everything became more and more uncertain. As I lay in bed at night staring at the ceiling fan, my small family had never seemed more fragile or vulnerable.

There followed a time of forced exile in the British colony for the family. Then in November 1941 a meeting of the Board of Directors of the Canton Trust Company was called. It was decided that the company should be relocated from Hong Kong office to Kweilin, and I was to oversee the transfer. Kweilin was chosen because of its location in the far northeast of Guangxi province. The board felt that its position at the most northerly point of southern China would offer safe harbor for the company and a secure base from which it could direct operations. It seemed sensible for Belle and the children to remain in Hong Kong until I found us a new home in Kweilin. Once that was settled, they could join me.

Belle was helping me pack my bags for the airline trip on the morning of December 3, 1941, when a strange mood overcame me. My previous trips away from home had filled me with anticipation; visiting a new city was always an adventure. Yet this time I felt different. For one thing, Huey, my oldest boy, was out of sorts and didn't want me to leave. Every time my going away was mentioned, he would cry. Huey, now six, was a sweet-natured boy, very mechanically minded, often lost in his own world of finding out how things worked. He loved to pull things apart, though he wasn't always good at putting them back together again. What I loved about him was that, beneath the bravado of being a little man, he had a sensitive nature and he liked having his father nearby. He would always glance over at me for approval and encouragement on whatever he was doing. He reminded me of the boy I had once been, craving a father who would never come. I understood what I was to him and I hoped he understood what he meant to me.

Leaving them, my little ones, Amy, Huey, Rudy and Yvonne, always drew conflicting emotions from me. I knew I had to balance my feelings with the practical necessities of a professional life. Yet, for some reason a voice inside my head kept on trying to tell me to delay this particular trip. Every instinct told me not to leave the family behind, to make any excuse I could and stay with them. I told myself not to be sentimental, that I would be back with them all the following week, that my job was the thing that was keeping this family together and safe. I couldn't have been more wrong.

My flight was departing from Kai Tak Airfield that evening. Belle came to see me off, and tears were streaming down her face when the flight was called. I was as troubled as she.

"Goodbye, Belle. I'll be back next week."

"Take care of yourself, and don't forget to write home the

moment you arrive," Belle replied, wiping the tears from her face. "The children will want to hear from you, Huey particularly."

It was dark when the plane took off, a precaution against enemy aircraft. I looked out the window and saw that the sky was bright with evening stars, and I felt sick at heart, thinking of my wife and children at home alone without me.

When the plane finally landed on Mom-Heung airfield it was raining hard, and the makeshift terminal and runway were flooded. We landed with some difficulty, with spray coming up over the aircraft's wings. We were all relieved to make it back onto the ground. As the downpour worsened, I made my way through the town's flooding streets to a run-down hotel that was still open to guests. After passing the night in that lousy hotel in Nom-Heung, I took a bus the next morning to Shukwan and from there caught the evening express train to Kweilin via Hang-Yank. After the train was delayed by two air raids, which forced it to pause until the threat of bombing passed, I finally arrived in Kweilin on December 6, 1941.

As I stepped from the train in Kweilin, that strange feeling possessed me again. I felt that I had made a terrible mistake leaving my family behind. I had an overwhelming urge to get back on the train. I wanted to run back to Hong Kong and get my family out of there while I could. I took a breath and told myself not to be paranoid, but the sick feeling in the pit of my stomach stayed with me all the way to the hotel. After checking in, I went to my room and used the bathroom, and as I stood above the toilet bowl, I looked down and saw that my urine was filled with blood. I had no other symptoms, no kidney problems. I considered going to the doctor, but it cleared up as quickly as it had come. I believe to this day that it was a warning from my subconscious mind. I went to bed that night but couldn't sleep.

One day later, on December 7, 1941, Pearl Harbor was attacked by two waves of Japanese fighters, bombers and torpedo planes—more than 350 in all—launched from six aircraft carriers. America was now at war with Japan. Less than twenty-four hours later, on the morning of December 8, while I was on my way to sign a construction contract between the Chinese Air Force and the International Engineering Company, I heard wild rumors that the Japanese had begun air raids on the British colony of Hong Kong. I couldn't believe it at first. How could it be? Walking into the hotel where General Wong was staying in Kweilin, I saw a huddled group of Air Force officers talking gravely with the general. The rumors were true. I had just left my family alone and defenseless, hundreds of miles away.

The general and I talked into the evening. He was also worried, his family also stranded in Hong Kong. We were hoping against hope that the city would hold out, but what if the Japanese took it? The situation seemed to worsen by the hour and I dreaded the cries of newsboys announcing the latest edition, but I would always rush to buy the papers and read the worsening headlines. One article said that the

Hong Kong government had taken steps to evacuate the population, especially the women and children, into the surrounding mountains. I was terrified for Belle and the children, imagining them in the crowds of refugees heading into those malaria-infested mountains. Who would feed them there? They would be on the road to certain death through sickness or starvation. It was only a matter of time. My mind was spinning with possibilities.

Three days had now passed since the attack on Hong Kong and I still had no news of my family. Travel back to the city was impossible. I had spent more than $200 in cable charges trying to reach Belle when I bumped into Captain Ding Kee Chui, who had piloted the last Eurasia plane to Kweilin, at my hotel. The local press had just reported that Kowloon, across the water from Hong Kong, had fallen to the Japanese.

"Mr. Kwan Wing took General Wong's and Odd Lim's families out of Kowloon into Hong Kong yesterday," said the pilot.

"What about my family?"

"I hope they are with them. I can't be sure."

Within the hour, radios seemed to be playing in every store, restaurant and hotel lobby. People had stopped working and now stood huddled solemnly together as newscasters relayed the breaking news in cold, grave tones. Over thirty thousand people had been killed in Hong Kong by the Japanese bombing and reports were coming in of twenty thousand more on the brink of death through hunger and thirst. The thought of my little ones starving and dying without me was beyond bearing. I fell to my knees on the hotel room floor and prayed. I had no one else to turn to. When I woke the next morning, I was lying on the floor, still in my clothes. I had fallen asleep praying.

Day after day of silence passed. The waiting was an agonized half-life where every detail of an ordinary day seemed suddenly remote, belonging to a world I was no longer living in. Hearing the birdsong of finches in cages or the clattering noises of crates being delivered in the marketplace, seeing the harsh yellows and whites of flowers in shop windows, listening to the cheerful laughter coming from tearooms, it was too much for me. I wanted silence. I wanted my world cast in black shadow, a half-light that my eyes could bear until I had my children safely in my arms once more.

I hadn't forgotten the stories that had come out of Nanking. The six-week occupation of that city from December 13, 1937, during the Second Sino–Japanese war was one of the bloodiest atrocities in Chinese history. It was impossible to know the real numbers of the dead, but what was for sure was that hundreds of thousands of Chinese civilians and captured soldiers had been executed by Japanese troops and tens of thousands of men, women and children raped. It was a bestial moment of inhumanity and medieval savagery. And now my wife and children were at the mercy of those same Imperial forces.

Then, on Christmas Eve 1941, came the worst news of

all. Hong Kong, once the jewel of the British Empire, had capitulated. A century of British rule had been brought to a swift and bloody end, and somewhere out there, beyond my sight but not beyond my heart, my loved ones were wandering, lost to me.

11

THREE HUNDRED MILES

Children, after the war, your mother told me in great detail the story of what happened after I left Hong Kong that day. I have done my best here to recollect all she said.

Belle watched my plane take off and went home. She too had a feeling of unease. She knew that the plan was for the family to join me in Kweilin the moment I found a house. The next morning, after a difficult night, she was relieved to receive my cable telling her of my safe arrival.

A couple more days passed. Belle had just waved Amy off to school one morning and was dressing Huey for the day when the first air-raid sirens screamed out their warning across the city. The sirens were soon followed by the sound of bomb blasts coming from the direction of the Kai Tak Airfield. The war had come to Hong Kong.

After the sirens and the bombing ceased, the streets filled up with startled, nervous people. Air-raid wardens, policemen and other servicemen tried to maintain order, but panic set in. People who lived near the airfield desperately tried to find their way to safety, fearing another attack. Ambulances moved through the crowds taking the wounded to hospital and the dead to mortuaries. All over Hong Kong, soldiers were building barricades of sandbags and barbed wire on all the main thoroughfares as the British colony prepared itself for a land assault.

Putting the terror of the situation to one side, Belle decided to focus on practicalities. Her most pressing concern now was food to feed the family. They didn't know how long the supplies in shops and market stalls would last: she tried to stock up on food to see them through, but it seemed that everyone had the same idea, and soon the shelves were emptied. Within days, the once civilized colony was becoming lawless, and gangs of armed looters went from house to house taking what they wanted and killing anyone who resisted. The nighttime streets became extremely dangerous as civil control collapsed.

Because I'd planned to be back the following week, the cash I'd left Belle with to see her through simply wasn't enough for a sustained period, and there was no way of knowing how long this would go on. Belle knew that I kept some emergency cash in a safe deposit box at the Bank of East Asia in Kowloon, but no one was allowed to cross over; the money might as well have been on the moon. With four young children to feed, every penny and every grain of rice now counted.

One night, when the city was quiet except for the drone of air-raid sirens and the rat-tat-tats of the anti-aircraft guns, Belle was preparing to put the children to bed when she heard someone banging on our front door. A gruff voice shouted from outside.

"Open the door or we will kick it down."

Terrified, Belle gathered the children together and directed our housemaid to open the door. The housemaid hadn't even reached the door handle when the metal splintered from the wooden frame and the door was kicked in. Five looters barged in, each carrying makeshift weapons stained with blood.

"Who is the master of this house?" one of the looters demanded.

"I am," responded Belle.

"We came by order of the Japanese army to borrow things from you, and, if you obey our order, nothing will happen to you."

It was a lie, of course. Belle stood by helpless as the looters ransacked the house, taking everything of value. This had been going on for half an hour when one of the looters appeared from the pantry, carrying a half-full sack of rice on his shoulder. This sack of rice was all that stood in the way of Belle and our children starving to death. Belle took a deep breath and approached the man.

"Sir, you have taken everything we own; take it all, I don't care, but if you have any mercy you will spare the rice for my children. We will starve without it. I am begging you to show some mercy."

The looter stopped and stared at the four children clinging to Belle. He put the sack down, then picked up some newspaper and hurriedly used it to wrap a few handfuls of rice grabbed from the sack. He handed the newspaper parcels of rice to Belle, snatched up the sack and walked out of the house.

Another looter appeared from the drawing room carrying a batch of keys. He fingered the handle of a long, jagged-edged dagger that was shoved into his belt.

"Tell me where is your safe, or I will cut your children's throats."

"Please, there is no safe in this house. You have searched the place already and I am telling you the truth."

"Oh, yes. What about these keys, you liar? They're keys to a safe. I can tell."

He pulled the knife from his belt.

"These keys are for my house and safe in Canton. I am a refugee here."

"I'll kill the children if you are lying!"

The looter made a stabbing motion towards the family.

Belle pushed the children behind her, all screaming now as the man with the knife shouted that he wanted to know where the safe was.

"It isn't here, it is in Canton!"

The looter shook his head and threw the keys onto the floor in disgust as a third looter appeared from a bedroom holding Belle's white fur cape. It was a Christmas present I had bought her several years before.

"You have no money, eh? I suppose this isn't yours?"

"Yes, the cape is mine, but it is not a new one. I brought this down from Canton. As I told your colleague here, we are refugees. Also, please, could you tell me what the Japanese army want with a lady's fur cape? Are they planning on dressing up for a dance to celebrate their victory over the British?"

The looters laughed and left.

As the Japanese advanced on Kowloon and Hong Kong, people bolted their doors tight and stayed off the streets, hoping to stay safe, but Belle's food situation was now precarious. Trying to eke out what little rice they had left, she made the children a plain and thin congee. But as days went by, the handfuls of rice they had left diminished. Venturing out onto the streets to find food was now a risk a mother would have to take to keep her babies alive.

When Hong Kong finally fell, the new Japanese governor of the former British colony asked the local people to cooperate with the Japanese army. With the streets controlled by occupying soldiers, some order returned, but one risk had been exchanged for another. Without food or access to money to buy it, Belle slowly realized that she would soon have no alternative but to escape Hong Kong with the children.

Her plan was simply to head towards me in Kweilin. If she could get past the Japanese lines and patrols without being molested or worse, it meant a journey of some 322 miles by foot through harsh terrain with four small children. It seemed impossible, but the choice was stark: walk or starve.

She asked a friend of the family, a Mr. Kwan, for advice.

"You will have to wait until the Japs allow us access to your safety deposit box," he said. "You will need all your jewelry, cash and goods to barter for food along the way."

"How long do you think we have to wait for that to happen?" asked Belle.

"Probably two or three months," Kwan answered.

"Two or three months! We'll have starved to death by that time. I'm not going to wait for the Japanese governor's permission for anything. We'll leave next week. I don't have much money left, but we have to try. To stay is a death sentence."

When Belle got back to the house I'd rented for her and the children, she stood outside the front door and wept. Only when she felt that all her tears had been spent did she get up the courage to go inside, putting on a brave smile for the children so they wouldn't know how terribly afraid she was.

That very evening, after the children had gone to bed, Belle heard the sounds of screams coming from the house next door. A group of Japanese soldiers had forced their way into the neighbors' home, cruelly treated the men of the house and forced them to watch as they raped every female, mistress and servant, young and old, who lived there. The screams descended into ugly, guttural sobs, punctuated by the casual laughter of Japanese soldiers joking together, and Belle had the children cover their ears and sing nursery rhymes to each other to drown out the horror. It was only a matter of time before the soldiers found Belle's house.

Early the next morning, with the sounds of the brutal gang rape still in her mind, Belle went out in search of friends who could give the family temporary shelter, somewhere safer, or at the very least some rice for the children. The babies had not eaten a meal, not even congee, for the last twelve hours and all the money I had left was gone.

Thinking that colleagues at the Canton Trust Company might be able to help, Belle went to see the bank's general manager, Mr. Y. T. Lim. He gave her a $100 bill, but the note was useless. The large bills had been driven out of circulation by the war, and no one would accept it. Desperate, she headed to see Dr. K. T. Wong, an old friend of the family. The Wong house, spacious and luxuriously furnished, was near Mr. Lim's home.

A servant answered the door when Belle knocked. The man smiled the moment he saw Belle, recognizing her from previous social visits, and asked her to wait there while he went to fetch his mistress. As the servant went into the house, Belle could smell roast meats, ham, eggs, bread, butter and coffee from a breakfast buffet. She was sick with hunger, and the smell of all that cooked food was making her feel dizzy. Leaning against the doorpost, Belle didn't see Mrs. Wong when she appeared.

"Oh, Mrs. Lee, what can I do for you?"

Belle recovered herself. "Mrs. Wong, I do apologize for the unannounced visit. Stephen, my husband, went to Kweilin with the bank just before the outbreak of war and has been unable to get back to us. Looters came, they took everything, all the food we had. The children have not eaten a meal since yesterday. We're old friends, as you know, and—"

"I'm sorry, Mrs. Lee. We have neither food to give nor shelter to spare for beggars. Goodbye."

The door slammed in her face.

Belle stood on the doorstep, unable to move through the waves of nausea. She listened to Mrs. Wong shouting abuse at the servant who had opened the door to her. When the nausea subsided, Belle turned and walked towards home, where four hungry children waited. Shaking with hunger, tears streaming down her face, she turned onto Prince Edward Road. She didn't notice the shape of a man quietly lighting a cigarette on the far side of the road. For a moment it seemed to Belle that he had been waiting for her. She put her head down and hurried on, but he called out to her.

"Mrs. Lee!"

Belle paused, a little scared.

The man hurried over.

"Mrs. Lee, don't be scared. Please. My name is Kan. I am a friend of your brother, C.Y. Do you remember me? Are you all right?"

Belle wiped her eyes with the back of her hand and looked

up at Kan's face. Though she couldn't quite place him, his face was strangely familiar; it was young, but there was something about his eyes she couldn't shake. They were kind, the kindest eyes she had ever seen, eyes that could have belonged to a much older man.

Kan could tell Belle had been crying. He offered her a handkerchief and a cigarette. She took the handkerchief and declined the cigarette.

"Mrs. Lee, what's the matter?"

"I need some money to buy rice for my children."

Without another word Kan put his hand in his pocket and took out a clip of $10 notes.

"I would give you more, but it's all I have. Take it. It's yours."

"But what about you?"

"You've got four children. And I have my cigarettes. I have a feeling that this will be my last pack for a very long time."

"Do you have enough money for food, Mr. Kan?"

"Feed your little ones and I'll make sure your brother buys me the biggest meal a man could eat, and a bottle of some very expensive brandy, when I see him next. He once did a great kindness, he helped someone even though he had no obligation to do so, and now I have the honor to repay that debt."

Kan pushed the money into the palm of her hand and closed her fingers around the notes. Belle was about to say something when he put his finger to his lips. He turned and started to walk away, then paused and looked back.

"Mrs. Lee, I will say a prayer for you and your family. Take care until we meet again and can share that bottle of brandy with your brother and husband. Hurry home and look after your children. I know they are missing you!" Then he walked off without saying another word. A good man and a good deed in a world of unspeakable suffering. For every act of cruelty, for every scene of horror conflagrated by the war, one single act of kindness seemed to have the power to restore, repair and give courage to even the most broken of hearts. Mr. Kan, wherever you are, whatever happened to you, our family prayers are still said for you; your kindness has not been forgotten.

Later, after the children had been fed by the generosity of Mr. Kan, the humiliation Belle had suffered in her quest for food finally overwhelmed her. Retiring to the bathroom, she wept out of sight of the children. She was a proud woman and had not experienced anything like this before. And some of these hidden tears were shed in the knowledge that this humiliation was just the beginning. Yet, for now, with the children warm, full, happy and sleeping after their meal, everything, for this moment, was as it should be; it was tomorrow that frightened her.

Two days before Amy's birthday, on January 9, Belle gave thought to what her elder daughter might like as a present; the options were thin. She had only a few dollars left from the money Kan had given her and a little rice left in the kitchen. Amy, about to turn twelve, was old enough to recognize how perilous their situation was, and she solved the problem.

"All I want is a bowl of congee, mother," Amy said, guessing at what her mother had suffered, "and for you not to worry so much about me. I am a big girl and I am here to help you."

Belle hugged Amy in her arms.

Later that afternoon, there was another loud banging at the door.

"Who is it?"

A wooden club crashed against the door.

"Open up, now!"

There was no choice but to obey, and the door was opened. Three tough-looking men stepped in with ropes, clubs and daggers.

"We are here on a mercy mission. Give us all your rice—or else," warned the first man.

The previous looters' visit had left the house devoid of anything of value and the rice was the only thing left. Amy, Huey, Rudy and Yvonne stood in the hallway watching as the men took the last bag from the kitchen. One of the looters spat on the floor in front of the children, he was so disgusted that they had so little to steal.

"That's all right, little ones," Belle said to the children. "We'll get some more rice by tomorrow, somehow."

But Belle was not able to buy or beg any rice the next day or the day following. The whole family starved together on Amy's birthday. With all the rice and money gone, the children went without food for two days. They were running out of options.

That's when Belle remembered that her former maid, Cheung Hing, lived in Kowloon. Belle's society friends had abandoned her and she had nowhere else to turn. So she packed up the children and headed to where she thought Cheung Hing lived.

The Japanese were now allowing families with children to evacuate to mainland China. From their point of view, it was better to create a refugee problem for the Chinese government to solve than to take on themselves the logistical problem of feeding all these people in Hong Kong. It would put a strain on Chinese resources and manpower while at the same time lessening the potential for civil unrest in the occupied territory. So Belle could now cross to Kowloon freely. She found the modest house and knocked on the door with our four hungry children huddled close. Belle could smell rice cooking in the background. When her former maid opened the door, Belle took a deep breath and spoke.

"Cheung Hing, my children are hungry and we have no where else to go."

Without a word, Cheung Hing stepped forward and welcomed Belle in.

Once inside the small house, Cheung Hing sat the children down around a fire, gave them each a small cup and put a spoonful of rice in each. The children ate it greedily.

"We'll see things through together. We have enough rice to feed us all for a little while," said the former maid. "You have us now. You are not alone."

The four children the year before their escape from Hong Kong—
from left, Yvonne, Rudy, Huey and Amy

After they ate, Cheung King gave the children a second helping of rice and poured Belle a cup of green tea.

"Cheung Hing, the situation will only get worse here," said Belle. "Food is scarce now. What will happen in six months? Our only hope is to get to the interior, to get to free China, where my husband is waiting. And that is what I plan to do in a few days. Why don't you come along? I would be grateful for your help with the babies."

"I can see that, Mrs. Lee. But my husband?"

"My husband will find a job for your husband, Wong Sun, I shall see to that," Belle promised.

Belle and the children stayed at Cheung Hing's house for a week while they made preparations to leave. It was the January 25, 1942, when they set out on the long and dangerous trek to reach free China. Their party comprised Belle and our four children, Cheung Hing and her husband, and a Mr. Fong Wing and his family.

Getting out of Kowloon wasn't as hard as they feared. The Japanese had little interest in women and children fleeing to the mainland. They weren't long into their journey when Belle saw that Yvonne, Huey and Rudy were far too small to make the trek on foot, so Sun attached two baskets to a long pole and put Huey and Rudy into them. He then balanced the baskets on one shoulder and carried the boys that way. Yvonne clambered up onto Hing's back while Amy walked at her mother's side.

The journey was slow and difficult. They slept wherever they could. If they were lucky, they would find an abandoned hut or temple that afforded some shelter. If they weren't lucky they would lie at the roadside, hungry and huddled together for warmth. There was little food and no means to buy any more. The children would often sob themselves to sleep at night, they were so hungry. Belle would try to comfort them as best she could, then force the babies back on their feet again the next morning. They had over three hundred miles to go before they reached any kind of safety. Every step of the way there were warnings of what would happen if they didn't keep going. The unburied, rotting bodies of children who had died of starvation lay at regular intervals along the roadside. Tales of the rape of young girls were rife, so Belle took the precaution of cutting Amy's hair short and making her wear boys' clothing to disguise the fact that she was a girl.

Japanese soldiers were everywhere. Sometimes they would surprise Belle with unexpected kindness and give the children some rice. Others could be dangerous and unpredictable. At one checkpoint, a Japanese soldier grabbed Rudy at gunpoint and took him into the guardhouse. Belle was terrified, not knowing what was happening to him. Rudy was kept in the guardhouse for two hours before the Japanese soldier finally brought him out, apparently unharmed. The soldier handed Belle a bag of rice, which she took, but she was scared to let the children eat it in case it was poisoned. We will never know what the Japanese soldier did with Rudy in that guardhouse, but he seemed fine; maybe the soldier was simply missing his own family back home.

The journey into the interior took months. Belle did her best to comfort the children all along the way, telling them that everything would be all right once they got to Daddy in Kweilin.

Throughout the journey, Belle expected cruelty from the Japanese soldiers. It was the callousness of people she believed to be friends that was harder to accept. The Fongs had been good friends before the war and Belle was pleased to have them with her for company during the journey. Mr. Fong had older sons with him and she thought they could help with the children. But they were only a few days out from Kowloon when Belle began to see another side to the Fong family. They had been walking for what seemed like weeks and one hungry day blurred into another. By the time they had reached Un-Long, Mr. Fong announced that it was his birthday and, using some of the money he had brought with him, bought enough food for a banquet. He then, with four hungry children watching, settled down with his family for a feast. How they could do that to four small children defies belief. Occasionally the group would happen upon a stall or a shop where some provisions could be bought or bartered for. Before Belle could spend what little money she had, Mr. Fong and his grown up children would barge in front of them and buy up everything that could be eaten. They never shared a grain of rice. The Fongs couldn't have cared less if my little ones had died on that road.

It wasn't long before the Fongs had abandoned Belle and

the children, pressing on with bellies full and not caring about the fate of anyone else. Belle pushed our family on, urging them all the time to keep walking. When there was no food, she filled the children's hearts and minds with hope. She would tell the children stories of how their mother and father met and what it was like on the day that each child was born. Every story had me in it; she made me the goal for each child. She made them believe that all they had to do was just keep walking, because one day soon they would turn a corner and I would be waiting for them with open arms, their father.

After hundreds of miles on the road, the family, now filthy, half-starved, skeletal and wearing rags, arrived on the outskirts of a town. The weather was cold and it was nearly night. Belle, scraping together a few pennies, decided that they had to find a place to stay indoors, somewhere the children could bathe and sleep in a proper bed for once. She saw a little hotel on the street and walked into the lobby, the children following. Standing at the front desk, she asked for a room. The hotel clerk shouted at them, calling them beggars and ordering them back out on the street. Belle tried to protest, but she was too weak to put up a fight. The weeks and months on the road had reduced my family to this: beggars. They were filthy, their hair was long, their clothes in tatters, and nobody had bathed in weeks. The night was getting colder, so, with Cheung Hing's help, they laid some blankets on the ground in an alleyway at the side of the hotel and the children shivered on the street for another night.

When they awoke the next morning, it was cold and the children were crying, desperate with hunger. Belle knew the end was near. Forcing the protesting children up onto their sore feet, she led them into town to see if she could find a street stall where they could buy or beg for some hot food. Belle had only a few coins left; she had bartered away everything she had brought out of Hong Kong, and she knew that her babies couldn't survive much longer. Starvation or the cold would take them. It was only a matter of time.

12

THE SEARCH

In the days and weeks after the Japanese invasion, I tried all means possible to get a message through to Belle and the children. A few of us pooled our money to hire a mercenary who might get messages through to our trapped families in Hong Kong, but the expedition ended in failure. Trying to get through the Japanese lines was too dangerous even for a mercenary.

I knew that time was running out for Belle and the children. Even if they had survived the initial bombardments and the Japanese invasion, I realized that my wife didn't have enough money to feed the children for longer than a couple of weeks. It had been weeks since I had had any news, and I knew the situation would soon be critical. That's when I made up my mind, as a father of four small children who needed me, to go back to Hong Kong. I had to find a way through the enemy soldiers and the fighting. I had to try to reach my family. My babies needed their father and I was prepared to die in the attempt to reach them. Resolved, I packed a few personal effects, including some traditional Chinese clothing borrowed from a friend who told me that the Japanese could be especially brutal towards Chinese wearing Western clothes. I paid black-market rates for a ticket on the train to Liuchow and set out. After an arduous journey, with the train stopping every time there was an air raid, I finally arrived in Liuchow and looked for a hotel. I had just lain down on the bed and closed my eyes when the phone rang.

It was a work colleague, C. H. Liu, calling from Kweilin. I had called him earlier to check in on whether there was any news from Belle and he was returning my call. He had news that set my heart pounding. Belle had been seen in Waichow. They were alive! My wife and children were alive! C. H. Liu's contacts had told him that Belle had set out for Kweilin by way of Shukwan. My astonishing wife, facing a desperate situation, had simply packed up our young family, risked the Japanese lines and led them on a three-hundred-mile trek to find their father. The strength to even attempt that journey with four children, little or no money, some trinkets to barter with and just the clothes on your back was beyond my comprehension.

A mother's love had carried four small children three hun-dred miles to find their father. They had walked and kept on walking with that one simple destination fixed in their hearts, and it allowed them to endure months of privation and suffering. They wanted to find me, their daddy. The moment I put the phone down, I broke down in gratitude. How many fathers really understand how much their children love them? How many men truly know that their children's love is a gift that can be lost forever if they choose not to nurture and treasure it? I had never felt less worthy of such enormous love and I had never felt more blessed. In my heart, I knew they were close. I had to find them.

Within the hour I had packed my things and checked out of the hotel, taken a rickshaw back to the station and boarded the very same train that had brought me to Liuchow. She was heading to Shukwan and I planned to meet her there. I sent a wire to C. H. Liu's contact to tell Belle, if he saw her, that I would be in Shukwan as soon as I could and that she should wait there for me. The journey took three days. On February 7, 1942, I arrived at Shukwan and booked into a hotel. It was only 3:30pm and I was exhausted after the long journey, but I could not close my eyes. I had no idea whether Belle received my wire. Lying down on my bed, I could hear a fierce argument in the lobby of the hotel below; the desk clerk was kicking a group of beggars out of the hotel. I could hear children's voices crying. It was awful. There were so many people trapped in a terrible situation and out there among them were Belle and my little ones. Sitting on my bed, all I could do was stare at the wall and imagine the worst.

The next morning I decided that I would go to the local Air Force headquarters. Maybe some old colleagues from my time in aviation could help me. I found an old-timer called Harry Chan, and we went to a teahouse called the Western Front to discuss my situation. Chan and I were still talking when someone tapped me on the shoulder. It was Dr. Chu Kwong Tow.

"Mr. Lee, your wife is here, in Shukwan, didn't you know? I saw her this morning. They were outside the Hoi-Gork floating hotel when I saw them."

I got up and ran from the teahouse. A short while later the Hoi-Gork Hotel was in sight. I could see them. Belle and the children were there. I shouted and pushed my way through the crowds towards them. The children heard my voice first, and moments later they were running, weaving their way through the throngs of people. Amy was the first to reach me, then Huey and Rudy. I was besieged by children. I picked all three up in my arms and hugged them. Looking up, I saw Belle walking towards me holding Yvonne. She was thin and gaunt, her clothes torn and filthy, her eyes wet with tears. She stopped and stood looking at me, and her mouth opened as if she was trying to say something, but no words came out.

"I understand," I said.

My words broke the spell, and she joined the children and put her free arm around me as Yvonne tried to climb onto me.

We were all crying and laughing. My little family stood there hugging each other for what seemed like hours. I didn't want to let them go.

"Did you receive my cable? You must have got it?" I finally asked Belle.

"No. The moment we reached Waichow we had to move again. The Japanese were always close behind. Lum-Gor arranged a truck to take us all here. If it hadn't been for him, we would have either starved to death or been killed by the Japanese troops."

I ordered a cab to drive us all back to the hotel where I was staying. When we arrived, Amy piped up; she was very cross with the people at this hotel and did not like them one bit. She stood there with her hands on her hips and scowled at all the hotel employees. Apparently, they had been very rude and called Mummy a beggar and thrown them all out on the street the night before.

"Last night?" I asked.

Amy nodded yes and pointed a finger at the desk clerk. That's when I realized whom the voices and cries had belonged to that I had heard. I listened to them, not knowing who they were, and did nothing. Half ashamed of myself and furious with the desk clerk, it was now my turn to be angry. I walked over and grabbed him by the collar, hauled him over the top of his desk and pinned him against it. The whole hotel lobby was silent and everyone was staring at me. The commotion brought the manager from his office, but I glared at him, daring him to take one step towards me, and he just stood there impotently watching the scene. The desk clerk was terrified and began to choke. It was then I realized that I had him by the throat.

Belle stepped up to me and grabbed my hand, telling me to let him go. The desk clerk collapsed to his knees, shaking and humiliated. There were tears in his eyes. Belle bent down and helped him to his feet.

"Would you like some water, young man?"

Belle glanced over to the manager.

"Some water, please, for this young gentleman?"

The hotel manager scampered off to fetch water. A minute later, as the clerk sipped his water, Belle straightened the man's collar. It was slightly torn.

"I can fix that for you if you bring me a needle and thread later."

The clerk looked at Belle with a growing sense of wonder in his eyes.

"Good, now, young man. My husband and I would like a room for the family. Could you kindly accommodate us?"

The clerk nodded.

"Excellent."

The clerk turned to go, then stopped. His eyes still wet, he glanced back at Belle and the children.

"I'm sorry, Mrs. Lee, I was just doing my job. I have a family too and there are so many people homeless on the streets."

"That's quite all right, young man," replied Belle. "Now

hurry along, the children are tired and in need of baths. And after we've eaten something, please remember to bring me that needle and thread."

I stood in the hotel lobby in awe of the woman I had married.

That first night in the hotel was the first good night of rest that Belle and the children had in months. After hot baths, Amy, Huey, Rudy and Yvonne ate a huge meal and then, with me sitting in an armchair in the corner of the room watching them intently, they and Belle slept soundly and securely, all huddled together in a double bed. That night the temperature dropped to below freezing. Heavy sleet pounded the same streets that the children had been forced to sleep on the night before. It was the first time in ten years the weather had been this cold. As I watched my family sleep, listening to the sounds of my wife and children breathing quietly, I could hear the sleet on the roof of the hotel and the tin-roof shacks nearby. They had made it just in time.

13

FLOOD

When we woke up the next morning, my immediate concern was to buy some warm clothes and cotton undergarments for Belle and the children. After breakfast, I dressed the children as warmly as I could in all my spare sweaters, shirts and undershirts and put my coat over Belle's shoulders. We must have looked like a circus troupe as we hurried to a local dressmaking shop. When we reached the shop, the manageress told us that because Chinese New Year was only two days away, they couldn't possibly have the clothes ready until after the holiday. My pleas that my children needed clothes went unheeded; the dress-shop manager couldn't have cared less. In the end, I had to pay her double to ensure the clothes would be ready for my family the next day. For the manageress, clothing for children, starving or not, was all just business.

On the way back to the hotel, the children, who were simply happy to be with me and didn't care if they were wearing my shirts and oversized sweaters, enthusiastically helped Belle and me to select the best melon seeds, Chinese sausages, preserved ducks, sweetmeats and firecrackers we could find, so that we could celebrate our first Chinese New Year in free China together.

After the New Year celebrations, with the children all proudly wearing their new clothes, Belle and I talked about where we should live. With the Japanese air raids now hitting Shukwan day and night, Belle wanted us to leave for Kweilin immediately, but I was reluctant.

The reason I had been sent to Kweilin in the first place was to establish a branch of the Canton Trust Company there. Yet the war had changed the whole economic landscape, and none of the old rules applied. It was even questionable whether our general manager, Mr. Y. M. Lim, still wanted a Kweilin branch. He was still in Hong Kong, now under Japanese rule, and the issue of establishing a new bank branch must be a rather remote concern when you have just been invaded. I had no way to contact him for instructions, and I did not want to move my family to Kweilin only to discover that the whole company had been dissolved.

"But do you think Shukwan is safe?" Belle asked.

"No," I admitted. "But it is still some way from the front. We just have to trust our luck and hope that the city stands until we've made realistic plans. They will give the order to evacuate if the Japanese are coming. We just have to be prepared to move at a moment's notice."

So we decided to stay in Shukwan, rent a house and put the children in school until the situation cleared up. We had some money and we were going to have to make it last until I found some employment. After ten days in the hotel, I rented a bamboo shed for $60 a month. It wasn't much to look at, but it meant I could use the little money I had left to feed us all a little while longer. The main thing was that we were together, it was warm, and the children, who had been sleeping in the open for months, thought it was a palace. The shed was located on the outskirts of Shukwan and near a school for the children. Unfortunately, we had barely moved in when the owner served us a notice to clear out in five days. He gave no explanation, but I knew why he had been so heartless. With Shukwan's population swelled to more than twenty times its normal size by refugees, rents had soared. If a landlord thought he could get more money for his shack, he didn't care if it meant putting a family with small children out on the street. We were a day away from being homeless when an old friend, a Mrs. Chang De Seng, came to our rescue and offered us temporary accommodation in her zinc-walled bungalow while I went looking for houses. Searching the city for somewhere to rent gave me a first-hand view of the endless stream of refugees arriving in Shukwan. The Japanese had driven a tidal wave of scared and desperate people before them, and with vacant houses almost impossible to find, there was no place for them to go.

A few days later, during a particularly heavy night raid, I found myself sitting next to Mrs. Chang and her family in the same air raid shelter. Without anything else to talk about except for Japanese bombs, conversation turned to the house hunt.

"Mr. Lee, of course you can stay in our house as long as you need. We won't see Belle and the children wandering the streets, you know that," Mrs. Chang said. "But I have a suggestion. Have you thought of putting up a bamboo-plastered bungalow? I know some other people who are doing it."

"How much would it cost, Mrs. Chang?"

"Oh, roughly three thousand dollars, I would say. That's what my friends are spending."

I thought it might work, but Belle brought me back to reality.

"Darling, how are we going to raise the money? We've hardly got anything left."

That was almost true, but not quite. I had the clothes on my back to sell, and that's what I did. I sold the most expensive pieces of clothing I owned, a Western-style tailored suit for $600 and a cashmere overcoat for $1,400—my last link to my previous life in banking. Then, with the help of Mrs. Chang, I found a suitable site and a contractor who said he could do what I needed within budget. To save money, I was going to plaster the bamboo bungalow myself. It didn't take long, and soon we had a small home.

Our little plaster-and-bamboo home was situated on a spacious lot on the outskirts of Shukwan, a five-minute walk from a school for the children. There was also enough room on the lot for our small house with a garden and a little yard for the children to play in. As shanty houses go, it was as comfortable as Belle could make it. She got the children working with her to plant corn, sweet potatoes and spinach in our small garden, which they all enjoyed enormously, and I was happy to see my family relishing the simple pleasures of home life once more. This little bamboo house with its four walls and small garden felt to me, for a moment, like a castle.

As the first shoots appeared in our little vegetable garden, the Japanese intensified their air raids on Shukwan and the bombing continued night after night. The Allies were being forced back all over Asia and great swathes of China were now in Japanese hands. But I tried to be optimistic. With the housing situation sorted out, I had gone looking for work and had been assured of a job with the Provincial Bank. Seeing the children put on weight again, I began to believe that we might just get through this.

Then one night in mid-April, when everybody was fast asleep, the mild weather turned, bringing with it a fierce gale. The violence of the wind was followed by a heavy rainstorm, then an intense flood. I woke when the first tremor hit our bamboo-and-plaster house. I got up and checked to see if all the windows were tightly shut and bolted, then went to bed again, but before I could lie down, there was a massive shaking. One of the bedroom walls collapsed, crashing down on top of the sleeping children. Pushing the debris away, I dragged them screaming out from under the shattered wall. Fortunately, they were unhurt except for Rudy, who had a slight bruise near his left eye. But we were now standing in the open air with a storm raging above us. As I pulled the children to me, the adjacent wall caved in, leaving us exposed on two sides. Some of our house still stood and we huddled together in its slight shelter as the storm tore our home apart, bamboo stick by bamboo stick.

Finally, morning came. As the storm began to subside, we saw that large parts of the town were now flooded with water knee-deep and our neighbors were busy trying to salvage what they could from their houses. Sampans were shuttling people and goods between the flooded areas and the dry main road. In spite of the disaster, people were remarkably cheerful. The war could do that. They were happy just to be alive.

As we pulled our possessions from the ruin of our house, the water began rising, filling the yard. We all carried what little we could up to the main road, which was already swollen with other flood victims' household articles, personal effects, chests of drawers, side tables, chairs, boxes filled with papers, vases, glassware, crates filled with books and trinkets, pots and pans and even discarded ceiling fans. Having salvaged what we could, we all sat together on the roadside and watched. All we could do was wait for the water to recede.

Night fell, and the flood tide was still high and strong. We could see our house from where we sat, and I watched in despair as the floodwater rose above its roof and swallowed the structure entirely. Hope seemed to fade as the house vanished beneath the water. It was all we had. Like everyone else on the roadside, we had no option but to head to a refugee camp that had been set up on a nearby hill above the floodwater.

We waded towards the camp but found all of the roads had flooded. The only way forward was by sampan. This was the first time I had ever been forced to become a public charge. I felt as though I had let my children down. Yet among the refugees in the camp I was surprised to see men who had once been rich and powerful, even some leading figures of the Chinese government. Rich men now slept on the ground where we slept and, like all the other refugees, had to get by on two bowls of plain red rice a day.

After a couple of days the flood began to subside, and those who could go back to their homes did. I went to inspect what remained of our bamboo house. Somehow, parts of it still stood. Walls could be replaced, but that would take time. Once again the wonderfully generous Mrs. Chang came to the rescue. Without a second of thought she opened up her home to my family again and told us we had a place to stay until the house was repaired. Three weeks later, two new bamboo walls had been erected and much of the water damage repaired. Our house was ready for us again and we all moved back, hoping that the worst was over.

It wasn't.

Not one week after we'd moved back in, news spread like a bushfire through Shukwan that the Japanese had broken through the Chinese lines and were advancing north towards the town. It was early June 1942. When the authorities nailed evacuation orders on all the telephone posts in town, it was time to leave. The same inhabitants who had been stoic and good-humored throughout the flooding were now simply terrified. We all faced a life-or-death decision: to abandon what little we had left materially of our lives, to leave behind that small security we called a home and escape the coming enemy, or to stay and face being butchered by the advancing Japanese troops. At least my family was with me and we would be together whatever happened.

As I was deciding what to do, I received a wire from Mr. Y. M. Lim, who had escaped to Kweilin from Hong Kong. He was calling a general meeting of Canton Trust Company senior management. So the decision was made. I packed up my family, carrying the few meager possessions we had left, and headed to the railway station. It was in chaos. The moment a train arrived at the station, panicking people, some with tickets and some without, rushed forward trying to force their way on board. I saw one man pushed onto the tracks by the crowds as the train pulled in. He rolled away just in time. The air was filled with screaming and shouting, the platforms packed with frightened and desperate crowds fighting for position. Above them, a voice echoed out of the tinny public-address system calling for calm. As one train pulled in, a fight broke out in a group of businessmen. People didn't care where the train was going as long as they could get on it. Standing at the edge of the chaos with four small children at my feet, I saw there was no way we could get through.

We were about to walk away when Belle spotted someone in the crowd she knew. It turned out that the stationmaster was a distant relative of hers. This kindly man took pity on us and helped us safely onto the Kweilin-bound express. It was an inexpressible relief to get on board that train. The children, the boys in particular, were in high spirits, thrilled by the prospect of a train trip, staring out of the train windows and chatting together excitedly. Belle, however, was quiet.

"If we had known that we had to evacuate so soon, we shouldn't have spent the little money we had getting the house repaired," she said to me as the train pulled out. I had rented our bamboo home to Mr. Lai Cheong for $200 a month, so it wasn't a total loss, but Belle was unhappy to be on the move again, leaving another home behind. She knew it wasn't my fault; she was simply frustrated and looking for someone to blame. I put my arm around her shoulders and told her it would work out. She didn't look convinced.

The journey was not a pleasant one. As the train made its way through the countryside we could see displaced people everywhere. The nights were the worst for the children. Other passengers, traumatized by what they had just lived through, would wake up screaming with night terrors. The conditions were cramped and uncomfortable, but we were happy just to be together and alive. When the express train finally arrived in Kweilin after two days and two nights on board, we went straight to a friend's house. A few days later we found a pleasant three-room apartment costing only $110 a month. As the weeks went by, colleagues and friends arrived in town almost daily, and familiar faces were seen everywhere, so much so that there was something of a party atmosphere as old friends were reunited.

General Wong, in Kweilin to collect his family, was able to attend the meeting that decided the future of the Canton Trust Company. With the hostilities making it almost impossible to continue operations, everything was put on hold until after the war. It was arranged for the company's employees who had made it to Kweilin to be given alternative employment at the China Industrial Bank, a commercial concern that was still able to operate in free China, and Mr. Y. M. Lim was appointed the new Kweilin branch manager. I was offered a new job as the assistant manager of the China Tea Corporation, which offered more money and better prospects than the China Industrial Bank. I decided to take this job, even though it meant eventually moving the family again, this time to Kweiyang in Guizhou province.

As I prepared to leave Kweilin, I was in two minds about leaving the family behind, but they were settled here. The children were in school, and I didn't have the heart to make them move again so soon. I also wanted to make sure the job was permanent before moving the family. This time, we had a contingency plan in case the situation on the ground meant the family had to evacuate again. Belle was adamant that she could take care of things.

"I'll be able to manage nicely during your absence," I recall her saying to me. "Just take good care of yourself up there and don't forget to write home often."

"I still wonder if it would be wise for us all to just move up to Kweiyang," I replied.

"No, I think the children should stay here as long as possible. We don't want to interrupt their schooling again, and if it looks like there is a possibility of the Japanese making it this far, we will come straight to you. We won't wait a second."

On September 4, 1942, I left Kweilin to take up my new post at the China Tea Corporation in Kweiyang. Getting a bus ticket was almost impossible, so I traveled with Mr. Harry Chan on an old gasoline truck provided by the Chinese Air Force. I'd seen a lot of Harry in Kweilin, and as he was headed to the war capital, he said he'd be glad to drop me off at Kweiyang first.

The highway to Kweiyang was carved and drilled through the high mountain passes, making it a nerve-wracking journey. With the truck laden with Air Force equipment, Harry, his family and I had to sit on top of the load, clutching hold of whatever we could. Sitting there, perched in the open air on top of the truck, we held our breath as its wheels careened inches from cliff edges and deep ravines, the groaning engine of the rickety truck rattling and coughing its way along the zigzag highway. Dreadful injury and death were as near as one tire blowout, and a single careless move by the driver could end in disaster for us all. From our bird's-nest perch on top of the truck's load we could see the wreckage of other vehicles that had plunged from the roadside into the gorges below.

The journey seemed endless, but after four tedious and constantly perilous days of travel we made it to Kweiyang. I was happy to arrive unhurt, but I was soon to discover that the truck journey was to be the most exciting part of my life in this backwards town. We were some five thousand feet above sea level and life there was as dull and dry as the weather. I missed Belle and the children and, as promised, I wrote often.

Dear Belle,
Missing you and the children terribly. Kweiyang is a very primitive city. It is the intersecting point between the trade routes of Kweilin and Chungking on the one hand, and Kweilin and Kunming on the other. This is probably the reason for its constant shift of population. People who have to travel between these cities are forced to go by truck, bus, or passenger cars. Air travel is almost nonexistent. As you know, the C.N.A.C. and the Eurasia Airplane Corporation's air fleets were destroyed by the Japanese during the Hong Kong war, and there is now only one surviving plane left from each company to serve the whole country. Truck owners and chauffeurs with cars are growing

rich. They are in heavy demand by the government since the loss of Canton and Hankow, and their pay to transport material from the seaports into the interior is extraordinary. The average money you can make on one trip from Rangoon to Kunming amounts to at least $10,000 per driver. And just think, the average salary for government employees is only $1,000 per month. The drivers can cover roughly four trips per month. Some I know have accumulated as much as $1,000,000. Can you believe it? Fortunes are being made simply by driving. This has led to the rise of a new class of citizen, Belle. We call them the 'driving class'.

Hoarding is the order of the day. Everybody hoards everything. Restricting the flow of goods into the marketplace is the best way to drive prices up. Government decrees are not strong enough to stem the tide. In fact, government officials conspire with greedy businessmen and merchants to take their cut. Their mercenary activities are responsible for the inflation China is suffering from—and here's the crazy thing. The same government officials who are in cahoots to create the problem have decreed that the solution is to print more money! To print more money that they can then steal from the people! Does anybody see this hypocrisy? Does anyone care as long as they get a cut? The problem is the system. The problem is corruption. Not the economy, which is only a math equation. Every schoolboy knows that two plus two equals four. In the Chinese economy's case, two plus two doesn't equal four anymore because someone has stolen the first two, charged interest on it and told everyone that it all somehow still adds up to four. Confidence in our currency has been shot to pieces. Soon you will need a whole sack full of Chinese banknotes to buy a pack of cigarettes. In the meantime, I am working hard and I hope the money orders are arriving safely. Use it wisely, and if you have anything left over, buy something that could be used for barter. Money may soon be worthless.

Daily I see thousands of our countrymen marooned and penniless here. Many of them sleep on the pavements and in various bus stations. It is an ugly sight to see them in such a pitiful plight. They are journeying from all over Asia to get home. Some of them have come all the way from Singapore, some from the Dutch East Indies, but most of them are from Rangoon and other Burmese towns. They have hiked all the way into Kunming and then by truck into Kweiyang. They are now waiting for transport to take them back to their villages in Kwong-Tung, Kwongsi and Fukian provinces. God knows how many died on their trek from starvation and illness. I have heard tales that some were even thrown off the trucks and left to die after they ran out of food or money or things to barter with. The British are doing their best against the Japanese in those territories, but the enemy seems unstoppable right now. Did you know that the expatriate Chinese community contributed thirty per cent of the total war cost? Now these same people are left to die at the roadside. The Chinese government just didn't give a damn about the people who bankrolled them. These poor people literally begged all the way back to their homes. What little aid they were entitled to receive from the government was squeezed right and left by the officials handling it, such proud sons of the Celestial Kingdom.

What has happened to people? Five days without food turns even the most civilized of men into savages of the worst kind. I ask myself, what would I do in this situation? Would I be the better man? Would I be able to accept hunger over barbarism? Would I be able to stay true to all I believe in under these circumstances or would I become as savage as these desperate men? We have taught our children about fair play, that everyone should get the same, that it doesn't matter who you are or what your background is. We tell our little ones that they must always strive to be good and kind, that stealing, under any circumstances, is wrong. This isn't something the world believes in, and what we're teaching our children is a lie. I've seen cruelty and corruption prosper. I've watched good men lose their lives and their dignity, incapable of competing in this Machiavellian circus, their prayers going unanswered or unheard. Would I kill and steal to protect my children? Would I become everything I despise if I went without a meal for five days? I hope I never have to answer that question. When I sleep at night I dream of a walled garden filled with trees, flowers and all manner of bright, new shoots of green and growing things. And in this garden you and I are sitting with the children and enjoying a simple meal. The sun always shines there. It is a place of birdsong, a place where we are all safe together surrounded by the dappled shadows cast by the swaying branches in the trees high above. If you dream tonight, join me there. Please give my love to the children and don't forget to take good care of yourself. I will write to you again.

All my love, Stephen.

14

ON THE MOVE AGAIN

Living in Kweiyang for three months felt like living there for three lifetimes. With Christmas only a few weeks away, my mind was with my family, and the loneliness of my day-to-day routine became more unbearable. Then, on December 15, 1942, I decided that I had had quite enough. I resigned from the China Tea Corporation. I wanted to be home with my wife and children for good. I didn't want to repeat what had happened to them in Hong Kong. The sleepless nights of worrying just weren't worth it. After I handed my resignation letter to the General Manager, he offered to transfer me to a better location if I would stay on, but my mind was made up. I wanted to be home with my family.

Spending the Christmas holiday of 1942, the New Year and the Chinese New Year with my family felt like one long celebration. The children were happy to have me home with them. It was far too cold for them to play outside the house, so I spent my days teaching them all the American songs I knew. They loved it, and our house was filled with music from morning until night. It was the first time we had spent so much time together as a family, and I have never been happier in my life. Rather than just lark about with the children teaching them songs all day, I also tried to help Belle with her chores around the house. She was happy for the assistance and would always praise me for my attempts at housework, then secretly redo everything when I stepped out. She didn't want to discourage me or to hurt my feelings. Our holiday time together was a wonderful time. This was how life should always be.

As we moved into 1943 I took a job with a local bookkeeping firm to pay the bills, but my heart wasn't really in it. My focus was spending time with the children; I'd nearly lost them and I was anxious to be there if they needed me. Later that year I was ready to start focusing on my career again when an opportunity came up to become the Kweilin manager of Hip Sing Cheong Construction Company. The central activity of the company was building airfields for the Chinese Air Force. The owners had become rich men with the lucrative contracts they had been granted by the government, and my experience within the Air Force could prove invaluable to the growth of the business. I was looking forward to starting when an alert came over the news wires of a Japanese push towards Hunan province in the south central part of China. It was May 1944. The news was swiftly followed by an evacuation order. Work on the airfields was instantly suspended. We were on the run again.

The original inhabitants of Kweilin had never experienced the grim terror of war or the stinging panic of evacuation. When the evacuation order came, the city was in bedlam. Very few people, including those who had escaped from Hong Kong two years ago, ever thought that they would have to leave this place. No one had believed that the Japanese could come this far inland, right into the heart of China. For Belle and the children, however, evacuation was an expected risk and they took it in their stride. We finalized our business in Kweilin in the most matter-of-fact manner and then made arrangements for transportation.

I sent Belle and the children to Liuchow by truck, while I stayed behind to finish some company business in Kweilin. I planned to join them the moment I could. Within days, though, I became sick with a severe case of dysentery. When the final evacuation order came on September 13, 1944, there was no choice but for me to stay behind at the hotel where I was staying.

It was touch and go, but after a couple of days I felt well enough to travel and made my way to the railroad station, where I paid a black-market price for a ticket and managed to board a train. Most of the population had already left the city to escape the advancing Japanese, so I was able to get a seat. It was small comfort. The train journey was deeply unpleasant. In normal times, it would have lasted only eight hours, but this time it took three days, and to sit on a train for three days with dysentery was almost unbearable. I had a high fever and severe diarrhea the entire time. When I finally arrived in Liuchow, I asked to be taken to the nearest doctor and had barely made it through his front door when I collapsed.

In a few days I had recovered enough to take stock of our situation. It was rumored that the Japanese would soon be targeting Liuchow. Not wanting to take the risk, Belle and I decided to pack up and head out. We weren't alone in this decision. The Japanese reputation for brutality with civilians was enough to get an entire town on the march once a rumor began that they were on the way. It was the usual story at the railway station: platforms jammed with desperate evacuees fighting, kicking, shoving and punching their way to get onto any train that would take them away from here. There were so many people trying to escape it was impossible to even get close to a train, let alone board one. The only alternative left to me was to take the family to Cheong On, some 100 miles upriver. The situation was getting out of control in Liuchow and people were frantic with terror when word came that the Japanese were closing in. Paying over the odds, I managed to secure us tickets on board a tow-boat leaving at 10 the next morning. I was still ill from the fever, but knew this was no time to lie down in a bed sick if I was to get my family to safety. I had to get my family on that boat.

I had lifted the last of my children aboard when I finally collapsed again. It was September 15, 1944. Belle immediately took charge, putting me in a berth and giving me the only medicine she carried with her, an antibiotic called sulfadiazine. My fever had now developed into pneumonia. I lay for twelve days on a bed below deck, in a cramped space tightly packed with other sweating passengers as Belle stood by nursing me. The boat was heaving with passengers, their luggage, and commercial goods. Without a cabin to hire, or a bed of their own, Belle and the children slept on top of our luggage. The journey wasn't easy. The waters turned to rapids in places, but we navigated them safely and made slow but steady progress. Midway through the second week I started showing signs of recovery as the boat approached Cheong On.

We reached our destination on September 27, 1944. Cheong On was a place in flux. The Japanese army's rapid advance was driving its population north. As in Liuchow and elsewhere, the authorities in Cheong On had commandeered all means of transportation, leaving everyone in a bind. After weighing up our options, I guessed that heading to one of the remote villages that lay farther upriver was the safest bet. I was advised to take refuge in Foo-Luke, a border village between South Kweichow and North Kwongsi. It was a remote place, accessible only by river junk. The dilemma was finding one that would take us at such short notice. That's when I remembered that the Air Force station was the most powerful representative of the government in Cheong On. I cabled General Wong for assistance and he immediately cabled back to tell me that I should approach the stationmaster for assistance and use his authority. Arriving at the Air Force station, I discovered that the stationmaster was an old colleague from my Air Force days, Mr. Au. Not that this mattered to Au; he was a crook who wouldn't lift a finger without money changing hands.

"Sorry, we've commandeered all the junks," said Au, lighting himself a cigarette. "They are held in readiness to transport our Air Force equipment vital to the war effort. I can't help you, Mr. Lee. The general can come down and see for himself if he is so inclined."

"And what would it take to cover the Air Force's expenses if a former Air Force colonel wanted to take temporary loan of one to go upriver? The junk will be sent back the moment we arrive."

"Fifteen thousand dollars," he said.

I pulled out $15,000 and gave the money to him.

Mr. Au counted the notes, pocketed them and said, "You shall have one ready by tomorrow morning."

On October 10, 1944, we boarded a lice-ridden junk and sailed upriver from Cheong On. I was still recovering my strength and Belle sought to distract the children by telling them that we were all on a great and magical adventure. On this adventure we would build fires on sandy beaches each night, cook delicious food caught fresh from the river that would be salted and roasted over the flames, and live like pirates. The children loved the idea of being pirates, of course, and Belle imbued all the new sights and sounds of the river with stories and characters drawn from her imagination, telling incredible stories of the monsters and heroes that now lived along the river and the travelers who had encountered them. This gypsy lifestyle, in some way, now suited the children. They were used to travel and embraced change, especially when the places they were visiting had been the stage setting for tales of heroes and monsters.

The family ate well on the junk. We bought meat and vegetables from the river villages we passed by. The older children were given the task of collecting dry wood and gathering it up into bundles ready to be burnt. Then, on October 17, 1944, after spending a week sailing, we arrived in Foo-Luke.

15

FOO-LUKE

Perched on top of a sand hill, Foo-Luke was a strange village. Two tribes of aborigines known as the Dong and the Mu inhabited it. The official dialect of the village was the Dong-Hwa, and the medium of exchange was Canton coins. Knocking on doors and asking if anyone knew of any accommodation to rent, I soon found a wooden shack in the middle part of the village. The living quarters were upstairs; the ground floor was a pigsty. What our ramshackle barn accommodation lacked in interior design it certainly made up for with the view from the windows. The most stunning scenery surrounded us, with wide vistas stretching across a verdant virgin forest.

Despite the million-dollar view, Belle said it would take barrels of Paris Soir to neutralize the smell of pigs and buffalo below us, but we had no choice. Frankly, a barn full of pigs snorting and munching peacefully on their lunch below was preferable to a confrontation with the Imperial Japanese Army. The children, especially Rudy and Huey, didn't care about the smell; in fact, they grew very attached to our grunting, peeing, defecating and occasionally windy housemates. The boys thought it was brilliant to be living so close to animals, and they soon started making up names for them and telling wild stories to each other of adventures the animals would have when everyone else was asleep. I had never seen them so enthusiastic to go to bed at night. They couldn't wait for the next morning, when they could ride the water buffalo down to the lake in front of our barn like a couple of Wild West cowboys. It was good to see the boys behaving like boys and having fun at last.

Foo-Luke was the biggest village in a district surrounded on all sides by miles of hills and mountains, broken only by silver streaks of river. There was barely a yard of road laid and hardly a decent house. Local tribesmen had made the few footpaths into the mountains so they could trade salt with other villages. A sampan journey down river could take weeks. If you wanted to journey by land, your only option was to use ponies if you could get them, which would let you pick your way through the hills and mountains. We were isolated, the conditions primitive, but we were safe, together as a family and away from the fighting.

I made up my mind to stay in the village for as long as we could. Our ultimate plan was to head to the relative security of the heavily defended war capital of Chungking. I thought we would have the best chance of waiting the hostilities out there. Foo-Luke was not meant to be a permanent base for the family, but a remote location that gave us a moment of respite from the war. We were out of touch with civilization and, to be honest, I thought that the civilized world wouldn't miss us. I was sick of its unfairness and petty savagery. Needing to occupy myself, I made use of my spare time by writing my thoughts on professional banking practice and accounting in preparation for the time I would step back into the business world. Belle experimented with the art of pastry making.

As weeks passed, the trickle of refugees from Liuchow and Cheong On going upriver to Yeong Kong or to the war capital of Chungking became a steady stream, then a torrent. The war, it seemed, was never far behind us. As river traffic intensified, I began walking down to the riverside each morning to look over the boats as they docked for supplies. I was hoping to spot some familiar faces among the passengers and learn a little of what was happening in the outside world. It was on one of these trips that I bumped into Chester Chow, Sit Gee Min and a few other old friends making their way to Yeong Kong to take up teaching posts at the newly relocated Kwongsi University. They had time to kill before the boat pressed on upriver, so I invited everyone back to our ramshackle barn for tea and pastries.

"Mr. Lee," Mr. Sit proposed, thoughtfully munching a freshly baked doughnut, "We are short of professors at the university. How about you joining us there?"

"I haven't taught for a long time."

"Don't worry, you're smart and well qualified in banking and accountancy practices and I can bring you up to speed with the curriculum," Mr. Sit replied.

I waited until my old friends had departed to mention the job offer to Belle. She was as practical as ever.

"If you have nothing else to do, why not? And I like the idea of being a professor's wife. It has a certain respectability my life has been lacking in recent months."

At that moment one of the pigs let out a particularly noisome expulsion of gas from below. Belle and I collapsed laughing. When we finally pulled ourselves together, I wiped the tears from my eyes and tried to sound serious. "But—the war capital. We'd planned to go—"

"Think about teaching, Stephen, it may suit you," Belle interrupted. "Business will always be there once the war ends."

I was still in two minds about going into academia when we heard that the Japanese were coming upriver, in spite of the difficult terrain, towards Foo-Luke. With the advancing troops forcing a choice, I decided not to take the university position but to head straight to Chungking. I was tired of constantly being on the run from the Japanese. All I wanted to do was to provide security for the children and Chungking offered that.

On December 3, 1944, we boarded a junk and sailed upriver with a group of refugees. We had made it only as far as Bing Mui, a small border village between Kweichow and Kwongsi, when we heard reports that the Japanese were ahead of us. We were sailing into danger. Immediately, we turned back to Foo-Luke. We were in a terrible dilemma. We could go neither up nor down. The Japanese army was rumored to be closing in on both sides. The possibility that the enemy troops might finally catch up with us was terrifying. Just when things appeared darkest, a report filtered through that the Japanese advance had been halted and in some places the Imperial Army was retreating in the face of a series of well-coordinated Chinese attacks. More we didn't know; it was impossible to verify. The general feeling was that the threat was halted for the time being, but I decided against taking any unnecessary risks without firm information.

Returning to Foo-Luke, we rented the only accommodation available, a thatched one-room hut high up in the foothills, an isolated spot with only a few other huts nearby. Shortly after we'd settled in, thousands upon thousands of battle-hardened Chinese soldiers began streaming through the Foo-Luke district on their way to war. Those soldiers were tough, rough and unscrupulous. They camped in any quarter, house, or hut, regardless of whether it was vacant or occupied. They were also potentially very dangerous and a law unto themselves.

One night we heard noises outside our hut.

"Open the door," a voice ordered.

The children were frightened. Belle answered.

"Who are you?"

I heard other voices laughingly whisper to each other, "Ah, women; we have women here."

They didn't ask again for the door to be opened, they simply kicked it in. I grabbed a wooden club, readying myself for what I thought could be a fight to the death. Belle just stood there, cool and calm, as ten soldiers in full battle dress burst through the door.

"Good evening, Sergeant," she said in Mandarin, spotting the rank on one of the soldier's uniforms. He appeared to be the one in charge.

Most of the Chinese soldiers passing through had been drafted or conscripted from the Northern provinces, so the fact that Belle could speak Mandarin was undoubtedly useful. Her father had been an official in the old Peking government, and she lived in that city for a number of years when she was a child. Now she saluted the sergeant, turned to the children and told them to do the same.

"Children, would you please salute these brave soldiers?"

All four children saluted.

"Stephen, offer your hand to the Sergeant. This may not be a palace, but it is still our home and therefore it is a house with manners."

The soldiers looked at the four children standing in a row saluting them. I had to admit it was a comical sight. They began to smile, then laugh. They saluted the children and laughed again. The Sergeant took my hand and shook it.

"Good evening, madam, sir and … little children," the Sergeant replied.

The four children, with Belle's encouragement, all piped up, "Good evening, sirs!"

Rudy walked over and offered his hand to the soldiers like his father. Huey grabbed his shirt and pulled him back. Instantly there was a scrap between the two boys. The sergeant shook his head at them, as if remembering something dear to him, as Belle pulled them apart.

"Boys, save the fighting for the Japanese," she said. "We're all Chinese here and on the same side." She smiled at the soldiers, some of whom were nodding in agreement through their laughter.

"I am sorry, madam," said the sergeant, who politely informed us that they were on their way from Hopei. "I can see you are busy and we hate to have been so … You see, we were tired and looking for sleeping quarters for our comrades. We've marched all day and needed somewhere to sleep for the night."

"Think nothing of it. You must all be exhausted defending our womenfolk and children from the enemy, Sergeant. Will you please come in and have a cup of tea first? It would be our honor to serve you."

Belle poured tea for the ten soldiers from the pot she had heating over a fire into the tin cups they carried. "We are refugees from Kweilin," she went on, "and my husband here is on his way to rejoin the Air Force at Chungking. He's a retired officer."

The sergeant looked at me.

"The Air Force?" he asked in perfect Cantonese.

"I was a colonel before the war, I asked to join up but they said they needed pilots, not accountants in their 40s," I said. "I was a comptroller. Logistics. They'll ask me back after the fighting is all done, to count and note down in triplicate all the bullets not shot at the enemy, no doubt."

The sergeant repeated what I'd said in Mandarin and his soldiers all laughed.

"If it had not been for you soldiers fighting so hard to defend the country, all my children here would have been killed long ago," Belle said in Cantonese. "Do you have children, Sergeant?"

The Sergeant nodded yes.

"We only have one room in this hut, but we would be only too glad to share it with you and try to make you and your men as comfortable as we can."

The sergeant looked around the tiny hut and at the faces of the children, all of whom were looking at the floor, except for one. When the sergeant's eyes reached him, Huey stepped forward and said, "You can have my blanket if you like, Sergeant. I want to be a soldier like you when I grow up and shoot lots of Japanese soldiers, so my mummy and daddy, Rudy, Amy and Nui-Nui will all be safe."

The sergeant smiled sadly. Then, holding his rifle in one hand, he knelt on the floor in front of Huey.

"I have a boy your age at home. He's a brave and kind little man just like you."

"Do you miss him?" asked Huey.

The sergeant took a deep breath; he seemed unable to speak. Without prompting, Huey stepped up to the sergeant and put his arms around the man's neck.

"He misses you. I know I would miss my father if he was far away fighting."

The sergeant ruffled Huey's hair and smiled. His men stood silent behind him.

"No, young man. The fighting is for me and my men to do. Your job is to look after your mother, sisters and brother and to grow up to be a good man. Then all our fighting will have been worth something. Can you do that?"

Huey saluted the sergeant.

The sergeant laughed, stood up and saluted my son back.

"Good, then you have your orders, soldier."

"Yes, Sergeant," replied Huey.

The sergeant turned to Belle.

"Again, I'm very sorry for the intrusion, madam, and I want to thank you, and you, sir, for the cup of tea."

The sergeant ordered his men out. He snapped to attention and gave me a salute, which I returned, then stepped out and closed the door gently behind him.

A few days after the incident with the soldiers, on

January 12, 1944, I heard another knock on our hut door. I opened it to find a polite young messenger standing there with his hat in hand.

"Mr. Lee, sir. The president of the University of Kwongsi sent me. He wanted me to personally ensure this was delivered into your hands." The messenger handed me an official-looking envelope. Inside was an official invitation for me to become a professor at the university teaching finance and banking.

"He said that if you were to accept, I was to escort you up to Yeong Kong at your earliest convenience."

16

PROFESSOR LEE

I had accepted the offer to become a professor at the Kwongsi University and we left Foo-Luke for the second time. On January 19, 1944, we arrived in Yeong Kong in Kweichow province, the temporary seat of the well-regarded Kwongsi University during the Second World War. Back then Yeong Kong was a small town set in a pretty landscape with a prosperous agricultural economic base. Rice, meat, vegetables and fruits were in plentiful supply, and it was by far the most pleasant place we had lived in since the evacuation from Kweilin.

The Japanese had already retreated from Dook Shan, which made travel northward easier, but the river, the principal route to Dook Shan, was still a dangerous place to attempt to travel with a family. Bandits and pirates had been reported all along the river. I wanted to head up there as soon as I could to resume my business career, but for now academia was the safer bet for a young family. By the time we arrived, what we thought would be a primitive outpost, far from civilization, had been transformed into a picturesque and bustling little college town. I enjoyed my teaching job at the university, and, more importantly, my salary as professor was enough to keep the family comfortable and free from worries for a time. After the upheavals of the last couple of years, the routine of daily life in a college town was a blessing. Should Yeong Kong be threatened by the Japanese, I knew that the university had an emergency plan in place to evacuate its staff and student population to safety. It was a relief to know that I wasn't alone, that there were others I could depend upon to help us.

The teaching staff of the university consisted largely of Chinese students who, like me, had studied in America and then returned home to China. According to the president of the university, this was the first time that the school was fortunate enough to have so many able and qualified men on its teaching staff. During my time there I met many American Air Force pilots passing through Yeong Kong on their way back to Kunming or Chungking. They were usually the survivors of bombing missions over occupied territories who had been rescued by Nationalist guerrillas. The American pilots were always surprised to find so many people who had studied and lived in America and spoke English fluently in such a remote region. They felt immediately at home among the professors; they would say this was the first time in months that they could use American slang and everyone got the joke.

It was now 1945, and as the semester came to a close, news broke that the Chinese army had recaptured Liuchow. It was cause for celebration. With Liuchow back in Chinese hands I figured that it would soon be much easier to get to Chungking. It was only a matter of time before the roads would open and air travel could resume. It would remove the risk of taking the pirate-infested river route.

I said goodbye to the teaching staff at the University on July 28, 1945, and took the family down river to Cheong On. Amy was attending Hon Min High School in Yeong Kong and we wanted her to complete the term before we took her south with us, so we left her behind in care of a friend, Mrs. Kwok.

Back in Cheong On, I was focused on finding out as much as I could about the condition Liuchow was in after the Japanese withdrawal from the city. I needed to make sure it would be safe enough for the family. One reliable and up-to-date source of information was the American warplanes that would occasionally short-stop at Cheong On Airfield on their way to Liuchow. We had rented a rickety wooden house near the airfield, and, given my background in the Air Force, we found it easy to open up conversations with the pilots who landed there. One afternoon, a transport plane landed on the airfield while the station master and all his staff were out drinking in town. I went over and greeted the American pilot and offered him some tea. After a brief chat, I asked if there was a chance of me getting a lift in the plane to Chungking.

"Sure, I'll be back from Liuchow next week. I'll land here and pick you up."

Within days of his offer, two atomic bombs were dropped on Japan, killing more than two hundred thousand people. No country could withstand that scale of slaughter. I was sure that the Japanese would surrender in the face of a complete annihilation. Peace would not be far away.

With the end of the war in sight, I made the mistake of allowing myself to believe that we were out of the worst of it, but I was wrong. The affairs of men are of little matter to a natural world that will sit passively by while atrocities are committed, wars are fought and civilizations shattered. Nature is her own mistress, and her voice, when she speaks, is louder than any cannon fire. When she comes in her full might she is a force like none other on earth, a power not constrained by conscience or mercy, sweeping away man, woman and child, the guilty and the innocent together. I watched as the storm clouds swept in over the mountains, rendering the sky a dense Stygian gloom. The whole region was blanketed by the impending storm, and within hours its full fury raged across the heavens for hundreds of miles, raining death and destruction on those who stood below. The storm flooded the Liu River in Cheong On, turning the river into a raging torrent that smashed its banks and destroyed everything in its path. All the major towns along the river were quickly drowned under the fast-moving water. Standing on the riverbank, I saw the most terrible sights. Wooden huts had been flattened and crushed by the floodwaters. I saw entire bamboo and wood houses uprooted from their foundations, careening down the river with their owners screaming from the windows. The river was full of the flotsam and jetsam of human life, people clinging to splintered trees, families trapped on the floating walls and roofs of their smashed homes, a single dog sitting, cold and shivering, on a log. As swollen bodies washed up on the riverbank it became clear to me that the storm had hit the area to the north of us particularly hard. With the flood still in full flow, my main concern was Amy up in Yeong Kong. It was sure to have been flooded, and I had no way of reaching her. All we could do was hope, wait and pray that she had made it through.

The storm took a number of days to subside, an unbearable anguish for Belle and me. As we waited for news, there was news of another kind. An American aviator on the way to Liuchow landed in Cheong On and told me that my prediction was coming true.

"The Japs are gonna throw in the towel pretty soon. It's gonna be over—the war is gonna be over."

If the Japanese surrendered, my plan was to head back to Canton as soon as possible with my family, but we couldn't go anywhere until we located Amy. I went out every morning, trying to meet people coming down from Yeong Kong, to see if someone had seen my daughter. The reports of events there, when they could be had, were terrifying for an anxious father. I kept this information from Belle.

On August 13, 1945, the telegraph office in Cheong On flashed out the news that the Japanese had finally surrendered. The war was over. At first the people in Cheong On did not take this peace news seriously. There had been too many false alarms in the past. It was only when the Air Force station posted the news from headquarters in the war capital that the whole town decided to believe it. They celebrated in the streets with firecrackers exploding everywhere. We didn't have the heart to celebrate V-J Day, though; there was still no news of Amy. I decided I could wait no more and set about trying to hire a boat to take me upriver, but nobody was prepared to head north.

Then, one bright morning, Huey, Rudy and Yvonne came rushing into the hut. "Daddy, Mommy," they shouted breathlessly, "junks are sailing down this way. Amy is on one of them! Amy! Amy! Amy!"

I ran from the hut, followed by Belle and the children. Sprinting down to the river, I saw a small flotilla of six junks sailing in our direction. I still couldn't make her out. The children were screaming with delight, shouting at the top of their voices and pointing. Belle and I strained our eyes but we still couldn't spot Amy.

"Where, where is she?" Belle asked Rudy.

"There! She's there!" Rudy shouted, grabbing his mother's hand and pointing at one of the junks coming towards us.

That's when Belle and I heard a weak girlish voice calling our names.

"Mommy, Mommy, Mommy! Daddy! I'm here! I'm here!"

Then finally I saw her, a small figure waving a bandana frantically in the air above her small head. It was Amy. My darling, beautiful little girl was alive and with us at last. I said a silent prayer of thanks and let the tears stream down my face. It was as though a knife had just been pulled from my heart—a heart that could now beat again because my daughter was alive. I picked Yvonne up in my arms and hugged her.

There was no holding Belle and the boys back. As Amy stepped from one of the junks onto the dockside, she ran through the crowds towards Rudy and Huey, waving her arms madly about her head to let them know she was there. Moments later, mother and daughter had reached each other. Belle grabbed Amy up into her arms and held her tight, weeping and laughing with joy. The boys surrounded both mother and sister with their hugs. No one was willing to let go of the other.

I walked down the dockside with Yvonne in my arms. As I reached Belle, Amy and the boys, I put Yvonne down. Amy glanced down at Yvonne and noticed something. Ever the big sister, she walked over to Yvonne, licked her thumb and wiped a smudge of dirt from her little sister's cheek. Then she knelt down and pulled up Yvonne's socks. They had fallen down, crumpled around Yvonne's ankles.

"That's better, Nui Nui. You won't get asked to the palace dance by a prince if you look like that," said Amy.

Finally Amy looked over at me, paused for a moment and then ran into my arms. I swept her up and hugged her. "Daddy," was the only word Amy said. It was the only word I had ever wanted to hear any of my children say. Even to this day it is the one single word that I still long to hear, the only one that matters.

Clambering off the junk after Amy were Mrs. Kwok and a number of others who had escaped the flood. Mrs. Kwok, normally so particular about her appearance, looked less than her usual smart and well-manicured self. It was clear she had been through an ordeal, yet there was something about Mrs. Kwok that made you feel she could cope with anything as long as she believed that she would have access to a decent hairdresser, manicurist and seamstress shortly afterwards.

Later, when we went back to the house to prepare food for our evening meal, Amy refused to leave her mother's side. She stayed within a few feet of her at all times. If she had been traumatized by the ordeal she had been through in Yeong Kong, she didn't show it. She simply seemed happy to be close to her mother again. I marveled at her resilience.

"Dinner is ready," Amy announced, carrying a big plate of roast chicken that her mother had prepared for the family, Mrs. Kwok and our guests. She placed it on our makeshift dining table and proudly stood there looking at everyone.

Behind Amy came Belle, grinning and happy, carrying two big plates of roast pork, bean sprouts and fried eggs.

"Yvonne, go into the kitchen and fetch the rice," yelled Amy. "Huey and Rudy, go get the rice bowls and the chopsticks and put them on the table, and make it quick, pipsqueaks!"

We all laughed. Our eldest and bossiest daughter was back with us at last.

Once we had all eaten, Belle couldn't wait any longer. She needed to hear everything, every detail of what happened in Yeong Kong when the storm hit. Mrs. Kwok, who had moments before been so relaxed, suddenly stiffened. She sipped her tea and took a deep breath. I indicated that she didn't need to say anything if she was tired, but Mrs. Kwok shook her head.

"No. No. You need to know what happened. But before I tell you, I want to say that this girl here, Miss Amy Lee, was a very, very brave girl. The bravest."

Rudy and Huey clapped. Amy scowled at them and they stopped.

"So. Where should I begin?" said Mrs. Kwok, a shudder in her voice. "I suppose with the rain. Yes, the rain. The rain began early one evening a few days ago. I'd seen monsoons and heavy downpours before, but nothing like this. Amy was in bed asleep and I had just started to fall asleep when, all of a sudden, a stream of floodwater came rushing through my bedroom. Only a few inches at first. I remember seeing my alarm clock. It was two o'clock in the morning. I jumped out of bed and rushed to where Amy was sleeping. She slept through the whole thing. Unbelievable! I dragged her out of bed and asked her to put on clothes and grab what she could. Minutes later we were outside on the street. By then all the streets were knee-deep with fast-flowing water, and it was still raining heavily. I made for the highest ground I could think of, a hill just outside of the city walls. When we reached the city wall, we found a large crowd gathered there, using any means they could to clamber up onto it to escape the rising water—ladders, ropes, whatever they had. The steps that led up to the top of the wall were filled with people, desperate people pushing and shoving each other. The wall is about twelve feet high, and people were using the top of the wall as a narrow walkway to head towards the hill outside the town. We stood, patiently waiting our turn to go up the steps, but with every minute that went by the water got higher and higher. The water was thigh-deep by now. Amy isn't tall and it would soon be up to her neck if I waited. It was at that point I thought, 'The hell with waiting, I have a child in my care!' I turned to Amy and told her to hold my hand and not to let go, that whatever I did she wasn't to let go of my hand. I told her that she would have to cling to me because her life was about to depend on it. With my other hand I barged, elbowed, hit and pushed my way through the panicking crowd, pulling Amy towards the wall and up the steps that led up the side. I am not a big woman, but I was determined to get us up those steps and get that child to safety. I am not proud of myself—I am ashamed of how I behaved—but Amy is here alive and if I have to answer for what I have done to protect her, then I will happily accept any judgment.

"With a struggle we made it to the top of the narrow wall. No sooner had we walked three feet than the walls, due to their age and the water pressure pushing against them, started caving in behind us. An entire section of city wall fell onto the poor people below. We had been standing with them only minutes before. The ones that weren't crushed must have drowned. It was awful. Amy and I missed that avalanche of rubble and rocks and mud by inches. If I had delayed a second more we would have been killed. But we weren't safe. Not yet. I could hear rubble and debris crunching into the wall we were standing on. The wall shook briefly, then stilled. We needed to move along that wall and get to the higher ground as soon as we could. I had no idea how long the wall we were tiptoeing along would last. At any second we could be tumbling down into the fast-moving water below. But ahead of us was a stream of men, women and children all making their way towards the hill. I shouted to them, trying to get them to walk faster, screaming that they had to move quickly if they wanted to save their lives. Babies were crying, and I saw one mother fall with her child from the wall in panic as she missed her footing. A man who was ushering his own family to safety couldn't let her die like that. I heard him tell his wife to take his children to the higher ground. His children cried out when he leapt off the wall into the water. He sank out of sight, then moments later he emerged from the water with the woman still clutching her baby. They were alive. His family were crying out to him, and he tried to swim towards the wall with the woman and her baby. He had only just reached the wall when a tree that had been uprooted drifted by. With one arm still around the woman and her child he grabbed hold of a branch and was swept away holding onto the tree. He called out to his family, but the noise and the screams made it impossible to hear his words.

"The section of the wall we were on began to wobble, but held. It was very frightening. People began to scream, some were frozen in fear. I kept shouting and screaming at the people in front of us to move it! Finally we made it to the far end of the wall where it intersected with the slopes of the hill. The ground there was dry. Soaked and cold, we climbed up the hill just in time to see the walls that ringed the city collapse with the biggest crashing noise I'd ever heard in my life. Many of the women and children we were with screamed with fright. But Amy didn't, she just looked back and quietly watched the city being destroyed."

Mrs. Kwok paused again. Belle held her hand.

"No, I'm fine, Mrs. Lee. It needs to be said. And once I've told the story, I will never speak of it again." She took a sip of water. "It rained for hours on end. We had nothing to eat and we were shivering from exhaustion, wet and cold. We had nothing else to do but to huddle together and hope for the rain to stop and the flood to subside. Then, at dawn, the rain relented. As the sky grew lighter we could see that the whole town of Yeong Kong was submerged beneath the floodwaters. Only the rooftops of a few tall buildings near the hillside could be seen. We were lucky to be alive."

Belle asked, "What happened to the man who tried to save the woman and her child?"

"The university had boats out searching for survivors, anything that could float and be piloted, really. I don't know if they ever found him. I pray that he survived, along with that lady and her child. He's in God's care now. He was a brave and good man. I wish I knew his name. So many people died in that flood. So many were lost."

We sat in silence listening. I went to a cabinet where I had a small bottle of brandy stored. Opening the cabinet, I poured two small glasses of brandy and handed one to Mrs. Kwok.

"Mr. Lee, I don't drink."

I held the other glass of brandy.

"Just this once, Mrs. Kwok. In honor of a brave man and in memory of the lives that were lost."

Mrs. Kwok looked at the brandy in the glass

"Let God and his angels guide their way home," said Mrs. Kwok.

"To his courage," I replied and drank the brandy down.

Mrs. Kwok looked at her brandy. She didn't drink it. I could tell she felt unworthy, having fought others to get Amy to the top of that wall. Belle took the glass from her and raised it.

"To you, Mrs. Kwok, for bringing my daughter home to me."

Belle drank the brandy in one gulp, then kissed Mrs. Kwok on the cheek. Mrs. Kwok began to sob, deep choking sobs. Belle put her arms around her and held her.

About a week after Amy's safe arrival in Cheong On, I hired a junk to take the family back to Canton. People warned us of the danger of pirates all along the river, but I was prepared to risk it. Canton was our home and I prayed that our house in Tungshan had withstood the Allied bombing. On the morning of August 25, 1945, our entire family boarded a big seagoing junk along with Chester Chow, my colleague from the university, and we left Cheong On. We sailed downriver as far as Shui Hing, where we had to hire an even bigger boat to navigate the Pearl River. The ruins of war could be seen everywhere along the river. In Wuchow and Shui Hing, I saw nothing left of these towns except for the smoldering embers of burnt-out buildings. The Allied bombing had been relentless. I had no idea what lay ahead of us in Canton.

17

RETURN TO CANTON

In the early hours of September 6, 1945, the *Shui Hing*, an inland river paddle steamer, slowly made its way towards the Pearl River delta. I was standing at the rail with Amy, Rudy and Huey by my side. Finally, in the distance, I could see Canton rising out of the sea. The towers and spires of the City of Rams cut the blue sky with jagged teeth. Its million windows sparkled in the sun. I couldn't speak. I could only look.

I had first seen this city eighteen years before. The world had been very different then. Now Canton had just been through a brutal chapter in its history. I was to learn later from eyewitnesses that its population had starved under the Japanese occupation. They fought to stay alive; desperate, they ate anything they could. After all the horses, cats and dogs had been eaten, some turned to cannibalism, and human flesh was sold on the streets in soup stewed up from the bones, skulls and marrow of infants, the ill and the aged. I wondered when I heard the stories whether a place could ever survive that history. Could new memories be made there and a better future built where goodness and compassion replaced such desperate inhumanity?

This was the world we had brought children into. But we were lucky. Our vessel was only the second one to reach Canton safely since the Japanese surrender. A steamer that sailed one day ahead of us had hit a magnetic mine that exploded on impact, and the death toll on board had been high. The steamer that sailed one day after us would be attacked by river pirates, all of its passengers robbed right down to the clothes they were wearing. We had been fortunate. We were still a family. A family that had survived. That was all that mattered for now.

Hours later, we anchored in the shadow of the Oi Kwan Hotel. Belle and I were sitting on the top deck of the *Shui Hing* watching Huey and Rudy. They had been born in Canton nearly a decade before and now, being boys, were leaning against the iron rails on the promenade deck guessing how tall the hotel was. Below deck, Amy, charming, graceful and now nearly sixteen years old, was in the cabin below helping seven-year-old Yvonne get dressed. All the passengers were refugees like us returning to their respective homes or what was left of them.

When permission was finally given to go ashore, Belle and the children stayed behind. They were to wait on board until I made sure we had someplace to go to. I figured that I would move around the city faster without four children and luggage in tow.

"Daddy, when are we going ashore?" asked Amy, holding her sister's hand.

"Everybody's leaving," said Huey indignantly. "Why can't we go along?"

"I am going ashore now to look up some friends in Sha-meen and see if I can find a place for us to stay until we can move into our house in Tungshan," I explained. "You are to stay on board with Mother for a little while longer until I return."

I spoke more confidently than I felt. First, I knew, I had to find out if our old home was still habitable or even standing. It could have been destroyed in an air raid from either side. If a bomb had leveled it, then we would have to quickly find somewhere else to live. Given that most of the population was still missing from Canton, though, I figured that a housing shortage wouldn't be one of the city's major problems. It should be relatively straightforward to find us somewhere to live temporarily. After accommodation, we would need money. I had to find a job, something that would allow us to live and survive day to day.

Leaving the children sitting despondent on the deck, I went ashore that morning wondering where my old friends and colleagues and business acquaintances could be found, not even knowing whether they were alive or dead. The Oi Kwan Hotel right there on the wharf was, I thought, a good place to start. Before the war I had known the manager at the hotel. I approached the clerk behind the front desk and inquired if my old friend was still in charge.

"I want to see the manager, Richard, please."

"Mr. Richard. Yes, of course, and who may I say is inquiring?"

"Mr. Stephen Jin-Nom Lee. I am an old friend."

A few minutes later Richard appeared. I had last seen him in 1938, just before the evacuation of Canton. Once good-looking and quite the ladies' man, Richard was barely recognizable, pale and thin with sunken cheeks and hollow eyes. He was touchingly pleased to discover that I was still alive after all these years. He held out his hand and as I grasped it I felt his bony fingers in the palm of my hand.

He led me to a seat in the lobby where we sat and caught up. Time was pressing for me, with my family waiting at the port. Understanding my hurry, Richard gave me a quick account of the current situation in Canton and told me he would do what he could to help me.

After wishing Richard a good day and thanking him for his time, I hired a rickshaw outside the hotel and asked the coolie to take me to Sha-meen. It was disconcerting to pass armed Japanese guards stationed at all the intersections. The city, by arrangement with the Allies, was still under the control of the puppet government installed by the Japanese. It made me feel very nervous; I had just spent the last few years being bombed by them.

In the days after V-J Day, the Chinese government had been concerned about looting and civil order. It simply didn't have the resources to take over the policing of major cities at the time of the Japanese surrender. Without an immediate alternative, it was thought better to have some sort of civil authority in charge rather than just let it descend into anarchy. So an agreement was reached between victor and vanquished: the latter was to be responsible for maintaining public order until the Chinese government was ready to assume responsibility. As a result, the Japanese still controlled the streets. It was a curious situation. One moment the Japanese soldiers were diligently trying to kill us with bombs, bullets and bayonets and now, with the flick of a switch, they were equally fastidious about managing our traffic for us.

The rickshaw eventually stopped in front of the F. Feld & Company building. I was pleased to see that the firm's sign was still hanging outside. Before the war, I had an expat friend who worked here, a German businessman called Fritz. My friend deplored the rise of the Nazis in his homeland, so he had stayed in China, happy to be as far away from Adolf Hitler as possible. I knocked on the front door and the firm's desk clerk answered.

"Mr. Lee?" said Ah Yoke, recognizing me. "Come in, please. When did you come back?"

"This morning. Is Mr. Lam or Mr. Fritz available?"

At that moment Fritz appeared behind Ah Yoke. He grabbed my hand and shook it.

"Mr. Lee, Mr. Lee. We are so happy to see you again. Well, well, how are you?"

The comprador, Mr. Lam, the Chinese manager of the firm, was due any moment. Fritz asked Ah Yoke to tell him Mr. Lee was here. Fritz then gave instructions to cancel all his morning meetings and led me into the reception room, where he offered me tea and biscuits. When he asked about the family, I told him they were waiting on a steamer at the port while I found temporary lodgings for us to rent. As it turned out, Fritz knew of a furnished apartment in Sha-meen, in the old US consulate building. The new landlord was called Kandoo and the vacant apartment was right below Fritz's friend, Karl, a former radio operator for the old Eurasia Airlines.

By ten o'clock in the morning everyone on board the *Shui Hing* had departed. The children were getting impatient, and Belle's anxiety had begun to grow as the time slipped by. It was Nui Nui, little Yvonne, who spotted me coming through the wharf gate.

"Look, Mommy—Daddy!"

Belle grabbed Nui Nui's hand and both rushed down the gangplank. I could see the relief on Belle's face as I told her my news.

"Fritz has arranged an apartment for us in Sha-meen. He says it's very nice and he's sure you're going to like it. Let's get going immediately."

It had been eight years since the Sino–Japanese war forced us to evacuate Canton. When we arrived in Sha-meen and the family was unpacking, my thoughts went to my mother. She had stayed in the old village during the war years and had very little news of us in all that time. It must have been lonely for her to know that her grandchildren were growing up and she wasn't there to see it. The war took us away from her and now we were home. I found pen and paper and wrote a letter to her. She had to know that we were home and alive.

The second the letter arrived, my mother grabbed a suitcase, filled it with whatever she might need, and set out for the city to see us. That first meeting after so long was memorable. She held each child for a full minute, and I was sure I could see her whisper a prayer as she did. And the children were thrilled to see their grandmother. They had missed her too. Nui Nui, being the baby of the family, was shy at first, but that soon faded. Within hours, she took to following her grandmother around the house whenever the opportunity presented itself and imitating everything she did. The rest of us would sing the Al Jolson song "Me and My Shadow" every time we saw them together, my mother with Nui Nui in close step next to her holding on to her dress or hand.

The Chinese Autumn festival was only a few days away and Belle wanted to celebrate the occasion. More and more friends and relatives were beginning to show up in Canton; this would be the perfect excuse to see them all. With my mother's help, Belle set about organizing a grand celebration.

The author reunited with his mother after the war, 1946

The family together in the late 1940s

On the day of the festival, guests and relatives began to arrive after the working day ended. Fritz, Lam and Karl all arrived together, followed by a stream of others. I busied myself as host, doing my best to entertain the guests and make sure everyone was introduced. Nobody was to be overlooked or not made welcome. Belle wore a Chinese black silk dress that she had made especially for the occasion, and I had never seen her more charming. Now in her late thirties, her girlish prettiness had been replaced with an exquisite, mature beauty and a strength and calmness of spirit. I was proud to call her my wife. I still am and always will be.

The dinner was delicious, yet the highlight for me, and the children who attended, were the moon cakes. Belle, an excellent pastry chef in her own right, had bought them from a famous shop in town, and they were exquisite. I had ordered some Mow-toy wine from the interior, which, together with the moon cakes, was sumptuous. During the years of hardship, an evening like this had been unimaginable. I have often thought back to this occasion and wondered whether the wine and food we served our friends were as potent as I remembered them to be. I may have eaten more expensive and exotic food since and tasted vintage wines from all over the world, but none, not a single crumb or drop, has ever held a candle to the food and wine we enjoyed that evening. After all we had been through, the simple pleasures of conversation, moon cakes and Mow-toy wine, well, they were as unforgettable as the famous Nat King Cole song.

Some time later, the Chinese New First Army arrived in force to take over Canton's administration. Officials, bureaucrats and civil servants soon followed. The city was once again under Chinese control. With life returning to normal, I had to think once again about the children's education. The war had been terribly disruptive and I hoped they could catch up, so I enrolled them in a nearby school. While the children were at school, Belle took the opportunity to visit Tungshan by rickshaw to check on our old house. She had delayed going there for as long as she could; she loved that house and knew she would be devastated if it had been destroyed. To her delight she found it standing, untouched by Allied or Japanese bombs. She was less than pleased, however, to discover that her home was still occupied by the Japanese army. The occupiers promised to return the house to her as soon as they received their orders to evacuate. It was the use that they had made of the house that I found most surprising. "They used it as a motor repair shop," Belle told me, waiting for my open-mouthed reaction.

It was hard to imagine our beautiful home as a motor repair shop, but that's what it had become. The Japanese soldiers had allowed Belle to take a look around her old home, and to her pleasant surprise she found it in better condition than she feared. Apart from the missing furniture, Belle thought that there was nothing that a few minor repairs and general redecoration couldn't solve. The bad news was that our financial position was precarious and I needed to move quickly to find a suitable job that paid well so the family could be supported. I hoped that the Canton Trust Company would resume functioning again as soon as the Chinese government re-established its authority over all the occupied territories, but I couldn't rely on it. There were some government jobs on offer, but I wasn't keen to work in that capacity. I had had quite enough of politics and petty officialdom during my time with the Air Force. I was still looking for work when Belle decided to take another trip to Tungshan to do a closer inspection of our house. As her rickshaw approached the YMCA building, a voice she had not heard in years called out.

"Belle!"

It was C.Y., her brother.

Belle jumped from the rickshaw and rushed into her brother's arms. It was an emotional reunion. Their parents had died during the war, and they had not seen each other since the fighting started. C.Y. was overjoyed to see his sister alive and to hear that all her children had survived the war. He had just arrived by plane from Chungking, where he had been appointed Special Commissioner of Economic Affairs for the provinces of Kwong-Tung, Kwongsi and Fukian. His job was to take possession and then dispose of all the enemy's property and assets in these three provinces. He was on his way to view some potential accommodations when he spotted Belle.

"C.Y., we have plenty of rooms in our apartment," she said. "I won't have you staying anywhere else. You can get to know your nieces and nephews; they've grown so much.

You won't recognize them! Stephen will insist on it, as will Huey and Rudy when they discover that their favorite uncle is in town!"

"I wouldn't want to disappoint the boys," said C.Y.

So it was agreed and they both took the same rickshaw back to Sha-meen, chatting all the way. C.Y. was amazed to find us already in Canton. He thought he was to be one of the first to return. But he was happy to be wrong and was even happier to know that Belle and her children were now safely back home. Belle was C.Y.'s favorite sister and he loved her dearly.

When they arrived in Sha-meen and opened the front door to our apartment, C.Y. was disappointed not to find the children.

"They are all at school, but they will be home soon and thrilled to find you here," said Belle. "Stephen is out looking for work. He needs to find a job or we won't be able to afford this place for much longer. There's a chance the Canton Trust Company will start up again, but so far, there is nothing definite. What little money we have saved up is practically all gone."

"I might have a solution," C.Y. said. "We'll wait until Stephen gets back to discuss it."

Later, when the children came home from school, they all dived onto C.Y., delighted to see him again.

"Children, I wanted to ask your permission," said C.Y. once the children had calmed down and were sitting around him. "I would very much like to stay with you all for a while.

That's if you don't mind?"

The children all clapped and cheered. They thought it was a splendid idea and wanted Uncle C.Y. to start his staying with them that very day. After living in the cloistered world of our own little family for years, the discovery, or rediscovery, that they belonged to a larger family who cared about them was a great gift to them all.

"I think that's a yes," said Belle, and the children all cheered again.

"Thank you, children. I would like to stay until my office is organized. Which means we're going to see plenty of each other from now on. Be prepared for lots of singing, fun and games. I even had a mind for us to put on a play for your parents. Something controversial," he said, winking at Belle.

There was more cheering from the children who thought that this all sounded like lots of fun.

"Well, C.Y., let's hope not too controversial," said Belle, shaking her head at her brother. He hadn't lost his sense of humor.

"What's *controversial*?" asked Nui Nui, who only moments before had been cheering and now obviously wondered what it was she had been cheering about.

"Are you going to explain this one, C.Y.? Or is this now my problem?"

C.Y. picked Nui Nui up on his knee.

"It means a play that will star a special princess who finds a magic wand. A wand that can, with one single flick of a wrist, turn naughty older brothers into great big ugly toads. And they have to stay like that, eating horrible houseflies all day, until they promise to be nice to little sisters."

If that was what controversial meant, then Yvonne certainly liked the sound of it. But more importantly she wanted to know when she was getting this wand. It was clear from the look she was giving Huey and Rudy, who were laughing at her, that she'd like to get some practice in with it right now.

"What about Auntie and Lucy, Uncle?" asked Amy.

"I shall send for Auntie and Lucy as soon as I have things settled. She and Lucy flew to Shanghai just before I left Chungking."

"Will they be bringing my wand?" asked Nui Nui.

"We shall have to see. That wand could turn up at any time. But only if you help Mummy around the house and promise to be the best little girl in the whole wide world."

When I got home, I was just as thrilled to see C.Y. as the children had been. After we had all caught up, I had news of my own to share with the family. I had just received a message from General Wong asking me to start getting things ready for the Canton Trust Company to resume business. There were a number of hurdles to be overcome, both logistically and legally, before its doors could formally open. But I was happy. Things looked as though they could get back to normal, and after the last few years some normality would be most welcome.

During the early stage of the Second Sino–Japanese war, C.Y. was instrumental in the relocation of industrial plants and equipment from key coastal cities into the interior. It was a bold and far-sighted strategic move to prevent the enemy from seizing hold of them and establishing a manufacturing base on the Chinese mainland. His audacious plan won support at the highest levels of the Chinese government, and one hundred percent cooperation from the businessmen in charge of Chinese heavy industries. If it had not been for C.Y.'s intervention, China's struggle with Japanese expansionist aggression might have ended differently.

18

BU SHIU DAT

As part of my mandate to get the bank back on the road to resuming operations, one of my first tasks was to re-establish legal ownership of the firm's headquarters. I discovered that the old Canton Trust Company building had been destroyed during the war and rebuilt. It in its place was a three-story office building. The ground it stood upon still legally belonged to the Canton Trust Company, though, and therefore the bank had a claim on the new building. It had stood empty since the evacuation of Canton and only recently been occupied by soldiers from the Chinese New First Army.

Obtaining the legal deeds to the land and the property was problematic, but not insurmountable. Enough historical evidence existed to back up the Canton Trust Company's claim to the building. The main problem was removing the current occupants who were billeted there. Negotiations with the officer in charge of the soldiers housed in the Canton Trust building were infuriating. He refused to divulge who his superior officer was, yet said that all negotiations had to go through him. I suspected the officer was stalling for some reason, and I was fairly sure money was involved.

"Will you please tell me where I can see your superior officer?"

"Bu Shiu Dat," they replied sarcastically. Bu Shiu Dat literally means "I don't know," and it was dismissive of me and my question. Chinese soldiers were never particularly tolerant towards civilians before the war. After the war, it was clear nothing had changed.

The situation on the ground in China was changing, though. Without a common enemy to unite them, the Nationalists and the Communists were now actively pursuing their own political and social agendas. Backed by Moscow, the Communists planned to take over the entire country, and the Manchurian provinces were the first to fall under their control. Seeing the threat, the First New Army, under the command of General Sun Lieh Jen, was given orders to head north to meet it. The soldiers who had occupied the Canton Trust building vanished almost overnight. Hearing the news, and thinking the building would now be vacant, I hurried over only to find that a newspaper-publishing firm was now in possession of the building. That was when I understood the reason for the officer's stalling tactics. He had made a deal with the newspaper firm's owner.

Undeterred, I marched straight into the reception and demanded to see the firm's general manager. He was not happy to see me standing there when he was brought out of his office.

"My name is Lee and I represent the legal owner of this building. A property you are now illegally occupying."

"This was the enemy's property," retorted the man who gave his name as Jang. "The Commission of Military Affairs authorized us to take it over and make use of this building."

He was lying. He knew it and I knew it. It was a stand-off. The fight to get the building back had just begun.

Corruption was as rife as ever and spread through every level of Chinese society. I had more evidence of this one late autumn evening when my German friends, Fritz and Karl, came to see me.

"Mr. Lee," asked Fritz, sounding embarrassed. "I wish you would do me a favor. Please could you keep this box of valuables safe for me?"

"And if you don't mind, Mr. Lee, I would ask you to do the same for me," joined in Karl, holding a miniature bronze chest of Chinese design.

"Gentlemen, I don't understand."

"We have information that they are going to intern all German nationals in a holding camp," Fritz explained.

"When they take us, they will simply help themselves to everything. If you don't keep these valuables safe for us, we will be left penniless."

"We have families to support and we know you are an honorable man, Mr. Lee," said Karl.

Fritz and Karl were two of the nicest people I had ever met, kind and decent to a fault. Everyone who worked with them respected their ethics and their lack of prejudice of any kind. They hated the Nazi party and what it had done to Germany. Internment seemed so pointless, vindictive and narrow-minded.

"Leave them with me, gentlemen. I promise I will take good care of them for you."

I took the two jewel boxes and asked Belle to put them in a safe place.

Shortly after the meeting with Fritz and Karl, I received a cable from General Wong in Nanking. The general had read my report on the illegal occupation of the Canton Trust Building by the newspaper firm, and he asked me to contact the Special Commissioner of Military Affairs, General Chang Fat-Fui. General Wong had contacted him already and ordered him to have the building's occupants removed immediately. I read the cable twice, then took a deep breath. While I assumed that General Wong and the Special Commissioner had the deepest of respect for each other, I doubted whether the people currently in the building cared much. They could issue order after order, each one more furious than the last.

The general manager of the newspaper-publishing company wasn't in the Chinese army and couldn't have cared less if they exploded with fury. The only way to get his company out of that building would be by way of a large bribe or at the business end of a soldier's gun.

The next day, I went to the office of the Special Commissioner and was met by General Chang's chief of staff, General Gum Lai Chor, to whom the general's request had been referred. General Gum was a stocky and gruff fellow with thick, bushy eyebrows and manners to match. His dishevelment was quite off-putting. Despite his general demeanor of dishabille, Gum showed me unusual courtesy in his conversation, but it soon became clear that this was as far as he was prepared to go. It all sounded like too much of an effort. Gum agreed to act only after I threatened to go back to the general and report him.

"I would like to thank you for the tea and the pleasantries, but I would trade them for some action in regards to the Canton Trust Building. You clearly plan to do absolutely nothing, General Gum. Now, I've worked for General Wong for years, and know him quite well, in fact. If he was to think that somehow the reason for your reluctance was tied up with financial impropriety—then I can't imagine he would be too pleased, especially if your gain was as a direct result of General Wong's loss. Not that I am for one moment accusing you of taking a bribe. But I could imagine the general leaping to all sorts of wrong conclusions after reading my report. General

Wong has a long memory and a short temper, and once he has made up his mind about something, then it tends to stay that way. And that means consequences. Now I am going to ask you one last time, are you going to assist me in sorting this mess out?"

That did the trick. Fear overcame Gum's apathy.

"I shall notify them to release the building to you, Mr. Lee. I am sorry that such a thing has happened. And please give my regards to General Wong. Tell him the matter will be expedited with all speed."

"I am greatly indebted to you."

The next day, I went to the Canton Trust Building and approached Mr. Jang.

"Yes, we have been notified on the matter," Jang said sarcastically. "We will vacate this building as soon as we can find another one to move to. We spent a lot of money getting your building into shape, you know. A great deal of money."

Mr. Jang wanted money and was not prepared to move out until he got what he wanted. The general saw no other way around Jang's intransigence, so I was instructed to return to see Jang with a bundle of five thousand Hong Kong dollars in a sealed brown envelope, even though it went against my principles. Jang took the cash, pocketed it and set about moving his company from the premises.

Even though the building was back in the Canton Trust Company's hands, we were still some way from becoming a formal business again. Without an income from the bank for the work I was doing to get it on its feet again, I still needed a job and a salary to tide me over. C.Y. came to my rescue and offered me a job with him.

Working with C.Y. in the office of the Special Commissioner for Economic Affairs allowed me to fully understand the scale of the racketeering being practiced by government officials behind closed doors. I soon discovered that the majority of empty buildings in the city that had been designated 'enemy property' actually belonged to refugees who hadn't made it back to Canton yet. It was only three months after V-J Day and 'Enemy Property' signs had been nailed up on practically every empty house and building standing. Organized crime was working in close collaboration with officials of the Special Commissioner's office, and it was business as usual for Chiang Kai-shek's government and its lackeys. There had been no change of heart, even though we had all endured a terrible war together. Where I saw suffering, these people saw only a financial advantage, an opportunity to steal what did not belong to them.

My job was to check and audit the enemy manufacturing plants and factories according to an official list submitted by the surrendering Japanese army. C.Y. wouldn't condone bribery or any other form of corruption in his office. He wanted everything to be done by the book, which suited me.

Touring the Japanese manufacturing plants, I was amazed at the pristine condition they were kept in, even after the war had been lost. The machinery was in perfect condition and it looked as though you could resume operations with the flick of a switch. I recall a cigarette factory, an ice plant, a sawmill, an oxygen and acetylene plant, a match factory, an alcohol plant and a dozen others, all of which could resume operations immediately. There were even stockpiles of raw materials waiting to be used. During the war I had developed a morbid dislike for all things Japanese—not entirely surprising given that the Imperial Army had just spent the last few years trying to bomb and shoot my entire family out of existence—but my job reviewing their industrial plants changed my opinion. You couldn't help but be impressed by their level of industrial organization and the pride with which they handed over fully functional factories to us. This spoke to me of a nation's mindset, its attention to detail, focus and innovation. I didn't think it would take too long for Japan to recover from the catastrophe of two atomic bombs being dropped on them.

My job with C.Y. took me as far as Macau and called for constant contact with the offices of the Special Commissioner of Military Affairs and the various administrative branches of the municipal and provincial governments. My close association with the officials who ran them soon revealed just how far these people would go to bully and coerce people into accepting their corruption. There was not a single case I reviewed in which ordinary citizens got a fair deal. It was very disheartening.

After the review of all the factories on the list was completed, C.Y. issued a directive to have them immediately put into operation. People needed jobs and goods, and we needed to stimulate commerce in Canton. I was appointed to run the sawmill, aiming to get it into production as soon as possible and turn it into a paying proposition. I knew nothing about cutting wood and even less about the operation of an entire plant cutting wood. While I tried to come up to speed on the postwar sawmill business, I learned that the Japanese soldiers occupying our house in Tungshan had finally been given orders to evacuate. The keys were delivered to me at work the very next morning.

Two days later, I received a message from General Wong asking me to get plans drawn up to refurbish the Canton Trust building. He wanted the bank to be open for business at the earliest possible date.

In early December of that year, Karl and Fritz's fears of internment came true. I was drinking tea one morning when half a dozen armed soldiers marched past my front door and stormed up the stairs towards Karl's apartment. Concerned, I went up to find out what was going on. I stood in the doorway and saw Karl silently sitting on a chair in the corner of the room watching the soldiers turn his apartment inside out. Their pockets and jackets were stuffed with everything they could fit in them. I watched as they took his fountain pen, his silverware, his shaving kit, his alarm clock, his shirts and even his neckties. I was about to intervene when Karl saw me. He simply shook his head, telling me not to interfere. I knew he meant that I should leave before the soldiers took an interest in me. Half an hour later, the soldiers led Karl away at gunpoint.

Because of my official position in the office of the Special Commissioner of Economic Affairs, I was allowed to visit Karl, Fritz and several other German friends at the internment camp, taking along baskets of baked goods that Belle sent and trying to supply a few luxuries that would make them more comfortable during their incarceration. They were kept in the camp for several months, then deported back to Germany once the paperwork had been processed. I was sorry to see them go, but happy to be able to return the chests filled with valuables to their owners. I knew that their contents would at least allow Karl and Fritz to make a new start of sorts in Germany. They had looked after me in a time of crisis and now it was my turn to repay the favor.

With our prospects looking better, Belle set about buying furniture and upholstery for our Tungshan house. She wanted it to be a home before she moved the children into it. My contribution was to invest in a piano, which I thought everyone would enjoy. I also invested in a second-hand Chevrolet sedan. With all the traveling I was doing between Tungshan, the sawmill and the Canton Trust Building, I thought that having a car would save me a great deal of time.

As one public scandal after another came to light, it became clear that people had grown tired of the status quo. The celebrations welcoming the Chinese government back at the end of the war had now turned to open resentment and anger. This lack of confidence permeated the entire economy, and our national currency was expected to go into free fall. People were ready for a change and the Communists seized the initiative.

They were extremely organized, distributing Communist literature clandestinely through sympathetic bookshops in the city. Communist agents exploited the hatred of the current government's corruption and focused the people's frustrations through propaganda, highlighting the problems and the failures of the current regime—not a hard case to make. People began to look to the Red Army in Manchuria to bring the change they so desperately needed; they gave little thought to the alternative society the Communists were proposing and what that would mean for them in the long run. They wanted change and were prepared to support the most organized solution that could bring about that change. The entire world was now one polarized by two opposing, well-armed ideologies. The situation even found its way onto the playground and into the worries of children.

"Daddy, my schoolmate told me in school that the Third World War is coming," said Rudy over dinner one night.

I told Rudy not to listen to that silly nonsense, but a voice of disquiet whispered at the back of my mind.

19

BACK HOME

By February 1946, the renovation work on our home was finally completed. It took three truckloads to move our household effects from Sha-meen, shortly followed by four truckloads of new furniture that Belle had bought. We were, at long last, back home in Tungshan. The trees I had planted before the war, on the western side of the house, had grown tall and graceful during our absence.

In my early days, newly returned from California, I never gave much thought to the Chinese New Year festival. Christmas was the big calendar date in the States. But the longer I lived in China, the more important Chinese customs and tradition became to me. As the Chinese New Year festival approached that year, the streets were covered with scarlet paper decorations and local shops and stalls were suddenly filled with melon seeds, preserved fruits and baked goods. You could spot ladies going into dressmakers to order special outfits while their husbands visited barbers. On every street corner you could hear children animatedly discussing the relative merits of firecrackers, firework bombs and squibs. This celebration, in everyone's minds, was going to make up for the last eight years of deprivation.

I remember that New Year's Eve well. Belle had prepared nine separate dishes for dinner, and as we sat around our family table, the noise of firecrackers all over the city drowned out our attempts at family conversation, but the children didn't care. It was splendid.

New Year's Day that year was a busy day filled with friends and relatives dropping by to hand out lucky money to the children. Belle and I went out early in the morning to do our own rounds so that we could be home in the afternoon to receive the friends and relatives who planned to drop by. By mid afternoon our house was full, and the two local women we'd hired for the occasion had their hands full serving tea, candies and melon seeds. As the day wore on, the guests drifted home and we could finally relax. It was not considered proper etiquette to pay New Year's respects to friends in the evening, and we hoped that this would be enough to keep anyone else away.

The sawmill was now up and running and we had begun

to turn a reasonable profit, thanks to the heavy demand from the construction industry for lumber. With the mill operating at full capacity, I was able to delegate some of my duties there and spend more time overseeing the restoration work at the Canton Trust Company building. I had always seen my future as being with the Canton Trust Company and I was eager to get the building finished so business could resume. With the end of the building work in sight, I resigned from my directorship of the sawmill and from my post as the Special Commissioner for Economics Affairs. I will always be grateful to C.Y. for the opportunity he had given me—the job came at the perfect time—but working for the government wasn't for me long-term. I wanted to be back in business.

The Canton Trust Company building was now fitted out and the interior attractively presented. Along with the preparation of the building, a great deal of paperwork also needed to be put in order before we would be allowed to resume business. This meant an application to the Finance Ministry in Nanking. We would only be allowed to start taking deposits and functioning as a bank once the approvals had come through. This necessitated a tedious series of applications and a lot of red tape to battle through. I was not happy to have to deal with government officials again, but I had no options. The job had to be done and I was the only one prepared to take on the challenge. Several board directors of the bank were in town, but all of them were noncommittal when the matter of assistance in expediting the applications was raised.

All they cared about was owning shares in a going concern. The general was the majority shareholder in the bank and its driving force. I was keen for it to remain that way. He was the only one who could control the other shareholders in the company, who I was sure would run the bank into the ground if it were up to them.

General Wong understood the amount of work I was undertaking on his behalf and was keen to assist me, so he had the complex application paperwork prepared by his secretary. When it was ready, he sent me a cable asking me to fly up to Nanking. He wanted to thank me personally. Getting an airplane ticket to Shanghai was tough because of the amount of postwar traffic. The only way was to pay black-market prices to jump up the waiting list, though I hated doing this. Belle accompanied me to the White Cloud airfield early in the morning. I remember the overcast sky and waving to Belle as I climbed up the steps of the big DC 47.

"I'll be back in two weeks!" I shouted back.

At the airport I found one of the general's personal secretaries waiting for me. Nanking—one of the oldest cities in China—was a place I hadn't visited before and as we drove through it I noticed how the old and the new jostled for the eye's attention. The architectural grandeur of Dr. Sun's mausoleum was especially striking.

The next day I delivered a detailed report of the affairs of the Canton Trust Company to the general. I was relieved to find out that he'd taken the initiative and forwarded the application papers to the Ministry of Finance through an influential friend of the general. On the morning of my departure, the general took me to one side. He wanted me to convey a message to the other shareholders from him.

"When you go back to Canton, Ah Nom, you can tell those guys back there that if they don't like my way of doing things, then they can either offer to buy my shares or put theirs on the table for me to buy."

On my return, we began the process of interviewing and hiring staff in preparation for the official go-ahead from the government. I looked forward to the day when we could simply get on with business, but it wasn't to be. A fierce argument erupted among the shareholders about the valuation of the shares. The problem was that the company's assets at that stage comprised primarily real estate and not one penny in deposited cash. Everyone had differing views, all curiously related to their own self-interest, on what a share was worth. I was dragged into this debate, and after several board meetings and much wrangling and negotiating with shareholders, a compromise was finally reached.

Once this emotional matter was settled, the board's focus was to set up the Hong Kong office. They wanted it open and ready for business as soon as possible. As luck would have it, Mr. Chester Chow, a fellow UC Berkeley graduate and Kwongsi University teaching colleague, decided to drop by the house one night. We chatted over a drink about his plans to establish an import–export business. Talking with Chester,

I thought that he would make the perfect candidate to head the trading side of the Canton Trust Company, so I asked him if he would be interested in coming on board. He was, and not long after, he was employed as the acting head of the Hong Kong office. There was less red tape and less corruption to deal with in Hong Kong, and by October 8, 1946, the Hong Kong office of the Canton Trust Company was up and running.

I had been lobbying General Wong to leave the Air Force and focus on the bank for some time. We needed him there on the ground to deal with investor politics. It was a welcome relief to see this cable one morning on my desk:

MY RESIGNATION FROM THE AIR FORCE ACCEPTED LEAVING FOR CANTON BY CATC TOMORROW.

At the next board meeting the general was unanimously elected chairman of the board and general manager of the company. One of his first tasks as chairman was to appoint the executive officers of the company. I was reappointed as the manager in charge of the Canton office. The government's official approval to reopen for business as a bank arrived shortly afterwards, and we officially opened for business on March 10, 1947.

Two months later, I was asked to go to Shanghai to open a branch office there. The bank was growing fast and I was having to work long hours just to keep up. While I was taking on more and more responsibility, my monthly salary of $280 remained static. I was barely able to cover my home expenses, while the shareholders, who'd done nothing to further the bank's interests or even see it back in business after the war, made the money. I was still brooding on this during a business trip to Hong Kong when Chester took me to lunch at the Cosmo Club. The moment he sat down, he could tell I was worried about something. I had begun telling him what it was when Freeman Koo, an old friend of Chester's, walked past our table and caught Chester's eye.

"Hey, Freeman, sit down. I want you to meet a friend of mine," said Chester.

Mr. Koo joined us. "My boss thinks he needs a better job," said Chester, half jokingly, as Koo sat down.

Koo was the second son of Mr. Wellington Koo, the Chinese Ambassador to the United States. Ordering a cocktail, he told us that he was planning on expanding the activities of his company, the Tien Yuan Industrial Corporation. He was hiring and my profile could fit the bill, but only if I could get by on the salary.

"We don't pay much," said Koo apologetically. "One thousand a month, but there is a chance for advancement and travel abroad." Little did he know that was almost four times my current pay. "You could be perfect. I heard from Chester that you got the Canton Trust Company back on its feet and even employed this old rascal here."

He grinned at Chester.

"Think it over. If you are half as good as Chester says you are, we would be lucky to have you. We're a great company to work for, Mr. Lee."

The next day, I went back to Canton and told Belle about the chance meeting and the offer.

"Are you going to take it?"

"I would like to, but I don't know how General Wong would take it. They would have to make me a firm offer in writing before I would even consider jeopardizing my current position."

"Well, since the general is paying you a pittance, he has no right to stop you from taking a position with a better salary."

"Of course not, but money isn't the only consideration. I have been associated with General Wong for such a long time. It may wreck our relationship. Is it wise to burn that bridge forever?"

"If you don't take that chance, you'll never know, will you? And, if he's angry at you for being offered a better job and salary while he's getting rich off your hard work, he's not worth knowing. Stephen, you are a father and have practical concerns to deal with. Four children to house and feed, for example. Putting food on the table is more important than General Wong's feelings. Or would you rather the babies went hungry just to please the general? He is a rich man and you aren't."

I was torn, but Belle was right, of course. And the difference in salary, and what that would mean to my family, made the choice straightforward. I handed in my resignation on

February 5, 1948. When the general received the letter, he immediately called me into his office and offered to raise my salary to $850 per month and give me the Hong Kong office if I stayed. He realized his mistake and decided to correct it. While the salary wasn't quite as much as Koo had offered, running the Hong Kong branch of the bank was a good career move. So I accepted his offer.

I arrived in Hong Kong in early March 1948 and moved into a dinky little flat on Wusoong Street that the Canton Trust Company used as temporary accommodation for its executives. I traveled back to Canton for weekends to see my family, and during the school holidays Belle would bring the children to see me in Hong Kong.

With the Red Army now openly fighting the Nationalist government in the north of the country, everyone sensed that change was coming. By the following summer the situation had worsened considerably. News came that the Red Army had taken complete control of the northeast of China and forced the entire New First Army to surrender. This was swiftly followed by reports of the six-month siege of Changchun by the Communists, in which some 150,000 civilians had starved to death. It was a glimpse of things to come as the Liaoshen, Huaihai and Pingjin campaigns ended in defeat of the Nationalists by the Communist forces. The Red Army broke the backbone of the Nationalist cause by destroying 173 government divisions. Over one and a half million veteran Nationalist soldiers were killed. The civil war was all but lost for Chang Kai-shek, and the Red Army's advance was now unstoppable.

The school authorities in Canton, sensing the end was coming, moved all examination and summer vacation dates forward. They wanted the students to finish the school year before their families were forced to evacuate if they needed to. Watching the situation worsen, I decided that Belle and the children should immediately come to Hong Kong. Being a British colony, it afforded us some measure of protection. But before I had a chance to arrange anything, I returned to my apartment after work one evening to find Belle and the children waiting there for me. Belle had pre-empted my decision.

"Daddy, do you think the Red Army will come to Canton?" asked Huey.

"Well, I for one, am glad that you are all here," I replied, not answering, although we all knew the answer.

The Red Army had crossed the Yangtze River and had captured Nanking on April 23. They were getting closer and closer. With its capital in Communist hands the Nationalist government was in the process of falling back to Canton. The Red Army would not be far behind them. It was the start of the rapid retreat that would eventually lead them to evacuate to Taipei in December of that year, abandoning the mainland to the Communists.

It was a tough decision for Belle to leave our house in Canton again, but she didn't want to risk being caught in the middle of a battle if the Nationalists decided to make a last stand there. Her decision to head to Hong Kong effectively made us refugees again; once again we had lost everything. All our security and savings were locked up in that house.

Looking back, it ultimately didn't matter. A house can't be a home without a loving family to occupy it. After all we had been through during the war, my priority as a father was for my little family to stay together no matter the cost. All I had ever wanted in life was safe and sound and with me in that modest little apartment that the Canton Trust Company rented for me.

With the decision made to settle in Hong Kong, Belle and I arranged for Huey and Rudy to attend Lingnam School, Yvonne to attend Pui Ching School, and Amy to attend Maryknoll Convent School.

"Why can't I go to Maryknoll with Amy, Daddy?" complained Yvonne.

"You have to finish at Chinese grammar school first. One more year. And then you can go to Maryknoll, Nui Nui."

With the family now permanently in residence in Hong Kong, we needed somewhere bigger to live, but the costs had skyrocketed because of the influx of refugees. The elegant house we owned in Canton seemed like a dream to me now, and I would sometimes catch myself daydreaming about one day living there again. But it was only a dream. After much searching, we finally found a more comfortable apartment that could accommodate a growing family. Taking a deep breath when I saw the price, I nonetheless agreed. On June 15, 1949, with our savings nearly exhausted, we moved into the second floor of 33 Maple Street, Kowloon. I borrowed some money to make the place habitable, which pleased Belle but left us both worried about the future. Even after we moved in, she was still worried.

"It's lovely, it really is. But how are we going to pay back the debt?"

I smiled, hugged her and told her it would be all right. Inside, though, I felt sick about it. If something happened to my job, we would be in a very tight spot.

I thought that a walk might do me some good, so I headed out of the building. I found the streets strangely quiet. You could see people huddled around newspapers on every corner. I walked up to one group, looked over their shoulders and read the headlines in the newspapers. It was October 15, 1949, and the Red Army had entered Canton the day before. One man was talking in a hushed voice.

"The Chinese Communists will be worse than other Communists. They reduce man to an obedient rubber stamp, a frightened sycophant. From the highest rank to the lowest, fear is the key to their rule. I have relatives in the north of the country. They all say the same thing. Anybody who utters a dissenting voice will be rewarded by a midnight visit from the security police."

The people listening all nodded and muttered in agreement. The man continued, "Everyone will suspect everybody else of being a spy. Mutual suspicion based on paranoia. Your neighbor could be betraying you right now. Everyone suspects everyone. It is brilliant in its conceit. Not even the fawning automatons will be safe. It is all about whispered stories of what happened to so-and-so. I am a schoolteacher. We will be the first to go. My brother is a Communist, we barely speak now, and he works in propaganda. What he does, they call it education. What I do, he says, is counter-revolutionary. Not agreeing is an act of treason. The Communists plan to beat, pummel and force this ideology into an entire population."

At that point, the man with the newspaper spotted me listening. We were in Hong Kong, in British-controlled territory, but people were still frightened. I tried to smile. Turning, the man hid his face and hurried away.

Mao Zedong proclaimed the establishment of the People's Republic of China and decreed that its new capital was to be Beiping, later renamed Beijing. The last pocket of resistance against the Communists was now in Taiwan, where Chiang Kai-shek and some two million Nationalist Chinese had fled. They declared Taiwan the temporary capital of the Republic of China. But none of that mattered. They were a spent force propped up by the Americans. China was now under Communist control.

On January 6, 1950, the British government recognized the Communist regime and withdrew her recognition of the old Nationalist government at the same time. This recognition brought some unexpected changes to the Hong Kong skyline.

You could see red flags fluttering on top of residential buildings put up by emboldened Communist supporters. Down on the streets the labor unions would hold rallies and make very vocal public statements in support of the Communists. Despite the seismic political shift on mainland China, the majority of the Chinese people in Hong Kong remained aloof and apathetic. The Cantonese had lived through a civil war and a world war. Everyone had suffered so much. The Cultural Revolution was just one more thing.

20

THE ÉLÉGIE

Ever since Belle and the children had come to Hong Kong, my mother's welfare had been on my mind. Living in a remote village, she had survived the war relatively unscathed, and I hoped that her location would afford her the same protection now. But she was getting older and I began to think about her long-term care. Getting messages to her in the village was now problematic, too. When a letter did arrive, it would tell me not to worry about her, that she wanted me to focus wholly on looking after her grandchildren. That was to be my priority. I remember one letter that told me that she was an "old woman who had outlived her usefulness" and that I had "more important things to do." She couldn't have been more wrong. I loved her and my children loved her. My mother gave up so much for me, and my deepest wish was for her to live out the rest of her life in happiness and comfort.

"Wake up, Steve," Belle whispered.

Belle and I had been out late the night before attending a party at General Wong's house and she'd let me sleep in.

"It's New Year's Day and the children are waiting patiently in the hallway, eager for me to let them in to see their father and get the celebrations off to a good start."

I could hear Yvonne whispering through a crack in the bedroom door.

"Is he up yet, Mummy? Is he?"

I smiled, rubbed the sleep out of my eyes and motioned for them to be let in. Belle opened the door. Moments later four children stampeded in, screaming with delight. They hurled themselves on top of the bed and on top of me. Amy had to help Yvonne up onto the bed. Nui Nui was soon jumping up and down on the bed shouting at the top of her voice.

"Happy New Year, Daddy!"

Belle stood at the foot of the bed, smiling at the happy scene. After each child had a big hug, she ushered them all out of the room to give me time to get up. She had just picked Yvonne up and was heading towards the door when she turned back.

"Oh, yes. Once you are up, there's a gentleman from your mother's village by the name of Mr. Cheong."

"Really?"

"He's waiting in the sitting room. I have given him some tea. He's come a long way."

I didn't bother dressing. I got out of bed, pulled my old cotton dressing gown on and went out to see the visitor.

"Good morning, Mr. Lee," said Mr. Cheong. "I am sorry to interrupt you on New Year's Day. But I have some bad news for you."

"My mother?"

"She is seriously ill at home in the village," continued Mr. Cheong. "I was sent by your cousins to tell you."

"Has she seen a doctor, Mr. Cheong?" asked Belle.

"Yes. It's dysentery," replied Mr. Cheong. "Two weeks ago she started showing symptoms. The local doctors have been attending to her, but the situation isn't improving. And now they won't come. Your mother ran out of money to pay them for their services and the medicine she needs. That is why I am here."

I couldn't speak. I sat down and took a breath. I was about to speak when Belle interrupted.

"It is very kind of you to come all this way to see my husband, Mr. Cheong," said Belle, going over to a dresser and taking out some money. "Here's $200 and some extra money for your transportation. Please take the money back to my mother-in-law immediately and make sure a doctor comes to see her. You have just enough time to make the three o'clock boat to Macau. And tell her, once I've sorted out the children's care here, I will personally come back to the village to care for her tomorrow."

Belle knew I couldn't go myself. My association with the old Nationalist regime and General Wong could present a problem for elements within the new government. I would face arrest if I went to mainland China. Belle was going to go in my stead.

Belle headed for the village via Macau on January 2, 1951. Although she had been back to the village several times since V-J Day, this was her first trip there since the Communists took control. She had no idea what waited for her in the new China.

Upon arriving in Macau, Belle took a rickshaw to the boundary post where the Communist border guards were stationed. She was shocked to discover that they were all teenagers. Not one of them could have been more than sixteen years old.

"Open your suitcase and take off your coat," ordered a thin, serious-faced young girl.

They rifled through everything and found an old Hong Kong newspaper that Belle had used to wrap some of the food she was taking to my mother. The serious-faced girl held it up triumphantly.

"So you tried to smuggle in anti-Communist propaganda, eh?"

"My mother-in-law cabled to me to say that she was dying. I was in such a hurry that I just picked up any old newspaper I could find to wrap these things in."

Under any other circumstances Belle would have laughed

at the absurdity of these children playing border guards, but not this time. There was something very different and dangerous about this group of teenagers. The serious girl ordered every sheet of crumpled newsprint to be burnt by an even younger guard holding a rifle and wearing a uniform that was too big for him.

"I will let you go this time," she said. "But don't do it again or I will see that you are hanged as a counter-revolutionary."

The girl kicked Belle's suitcase towards her, spilling the contents all over the roadside. Belle, retaining her composure, quietly repacked her case and hurried away.

When she arrived in my home village later that afternoon, she was alarmed to see how sick my mother was.

"Mother," she greeted her, sitting on a stool beside my mother's bed, touching her forehead with the back of her hand.

My mother briefly opened her eyes. Seeing Belle, she grew anxious and tried to sit up and speak.

"Don't try to exert yourself, Mother," said Belle. "Get some sleep."

Still agitated, my mother squeezed Belle's hand as if she was trying to communicate something, but she was too weak to carry on any conversation and soon drifted off.

Belle withdrew herself quietly from my mother's bedroom and went into the sitting room, where a number of friends, family and villagers had gathered. Belle was well respected and liked by the village folks, the children especially. She always brought them candies and cookies from Hong Kong when she visited. And for those who couldn't afford new clothes, Belle would always pack a few rolls of fabric.

"It is nice to see you all again," she said. "I want to thank each and every one of you who has given up time from working in the fields to attend to my mother-in-law. I know how much she means to you all."

The doctor visited that afternoon and more medications were prescribed. Finally, after a few days of rest and proper food, my mother started to feel better and was able to sit up and speak.

"How are Stephen and the children?"

"Amy, Huey, Rudy, and not forgetting little Yvonne, send you hugs and love. Nui Nui especially wanted to come with me to see you, but I said Lee Po needed to get better first and didn't need little people clambering all over her right now. I said she could come and stay with you when you got better."

My mother smiled.

"Tell Nui Nui that there is nothing in the world that would make her grandmother happier than to have her clamber all over me. Tell all the children that they are always in Lee Po's thoughts."

"I shall, when I return to Hong Kong. But we have to get you better first."

At that, my mother's expression changed. With her thin, frail arms she pushed herself up on the bed so she was sitting. Her face was flushed.

"No, no, Belle. You are not to bring Nui Nui or any of

the babies here. Do you hear me? Don't you ever bring the children back here," said my mother angrily. "I forbid it. Even if I am close to death and I will never see them again. You must let me die knowing they are all safe. Keep my grandchildren and Stephen in Hong Kong. You must do this for me, Belle. You must."

Belle was about to remonstrate. It couldn't be that bad.

"Stephen and the children will be watched the moment they arrive, and the Communists will never let them leave China or even leave this village. The Communists have already stolen all the rice we had stored, saying it belongs to the people. They had teenagers with them who sang a song I will never forget. The words were *Don't love Papa, don't love Mama, only love your country*. This is the start of something much worse, I promise you."

"It was probably just a silly song," said Belle. "You just take a good rest and I shall stay here until you get well."

"No, no," said my mother again. "I want you to leave for Hong Kong straight away. You should never have come. I would have stopped Cheong from going to see you if I had known. I am an old lady and my time is done. Stephen and those babies are the greatest blessing of my life. And those children need their mother."

"Let me wait a few days, until you are well enough to travel. You can come back with me. Stephen wants you to come and live with us in Hong Kong. So we can be together. A family. The children want you to come."

But my mother wouldn't hear of it. She ordered a housemaid to pack Belle's case and a cousin to carry it and escort her daughter-in-law to the bus station. Belle was unable to remonstrate. My mother was adamant.

"I will not be well enough to travel for weeks and then it could be too late. You need to leave now."

A few hours later Belle's bags were packed and she went to say goodbye. The old lady was sitting up in bed, holding one of the new photographs Belle had brought with her of Amy, Huey, Rudy and Yvonne. Belle watched my mother lightly touch each child's face as it smiled out at her from the photograph, as though she was wishing each child good night and sending a special blessing from Lee Po.

"Don't worry about me, Belle," my mother said at last. "Tell the children that Lee Po says not to neglect their studies, to be good children and to listen to their mummy and daddy. Take good care of yourself, Belle, and my Stephen. Tell my son that I am proud of the man he has become and all that he has accomplished. He has made my life one that was worth living. Tell him that he has been thousands of miles away from me for most of my life but, in fact, he was never more than a heartbeat away from here."

She lifted her hand and touched her chest above her heart.

"Tell each one of your children that Lee Po loves them. That their grandmother will always love them. Promise me you will tell them that, Belle? You must also promise me that you will never come back here, no matter what news comes. Never."

The family back in Hong Kong, 1950

Belle, wiping tears from her eyes, made my mother that promise. Then she left the old lady sitting alone in her bed, gazing lovingly at the photographs of her grandchildren.

My mother had looked into her future and, without a thought or regret, had put the needs of the ones she loved beyond her own.

When Belle returned to Hong Kong and finally walked through our door, she found the children anxiously waiting for her. I had already left for the office. Nui Nui was particularly worried about her grandmother and was happy to hear from Belle that Lee Po was getting better. She was especially pleased to hear that her beloved grandmother had sent her a special kiss.

In the days that followed, reports filtered back to us about my mother's condition. They were worrying. She had shown some improvement, then had a relapse. That's when the reports stopped coming. After a week of no news, I decided that I had no option. I was going to have to risk going back to the village myself. My mother was alone and I was her son. Belle had told me that my mother wanted me to stay in Hong Kong, that it was too risky, but how could I not go? How could I? After all she had sacrificed and done for me?

I had made my mind up to leave for the village when Belle opened our door to find a postman standing there, holding a letter addressed to me. As a rule Belle never opened my letters, but left them on my desk for me to deal with when I came home from work. She had quite enough on her plate with four young children to take care of. But this letter seemed different. She could tell by the postmark that it had come from the village. Holding the letter, Belle felt a terrible sense of dread come over her. She picked up my letter opener and sliced open the envelope.

It was February 21, 1951, and the letter had been sent, at great personal risk, by a cousin in the village. It was the worst possible news. In the week after Belle was ordered back to Hong Kong by my mother, a platoon of Red Army soldiers, led by a boy of about fifteen, returned to the village wanting to know the whereabouts of Mrs. Belle Lee, the wife of a well-known Nationalist sympathizer and close associate of General Wong. The general had fled to Taiwan with his entire family when the Communists took over and was a wanted man. The soldiers had orders to detain Belle for questioning.

The villagers told them that Belle had left the week before and was now back in Hong Kong. The soldiers would have left it at that, but the fifteen-year-old boy refused to believe the story. He flew into a rage, beating and slapping the villagers, saying that they were lying. He was sure that they were hiding Belle from him and that they needed to be persuaded to tell him where.

This boy had my mother dragged from her sickbed to interrogate her. In front of the whole village he ordered the soldiers to bring all the glassware from the house and smash it on the yard floor. Then he told my sick mother to kneel down among the shards, slicing her feet, shins and knees until the blood ran freely. He cried in a shrill voice that the villagers should tell him where Belle was hiding, that this was their last chance to tell the truth. Nobody answered.

Finally he waved his hand and ordered the soldiers forward. "Beat her!" he ordered them, and they began to strike my mother with the stocks of their rifles. "Beat her until the villagers tell me where the counter-revolutionary is hiding. Beat her!"

As the first blow came, my mother raised her hand to her heart and held it there. The blows kept on until my mother stopped moving and her body lay broken and bloody, face down in the shards of shattered glass. Checking to see if she was still alive, one of the soldiers kicked my mother over onto her back. She was dead. That's when the villagers saw what she held in her hand. In her still-clenched fist was one of the photographs that Belle had given her. As the soldiers beat her to death, my mother had refused to let go of this one special thing. She had chosen to die with a single black-and-white photograph of her four grandchildren pressed close to her heart.

Belle finished the letter, then walked unsteadily to the sofa in the living room, her heart breaking at the news. Towards late afternoon, she was still there, holding the letter in her hand, when the children came back from school. They knew instantly that something was very wrong.

"Mummy?" asked Rudy. Huey tried to take the letter out of his mother's hand, but Belle wouldn't let him read it.

When I arrived home from the office, standing outside the front door of our apartment I remember thinking that it was strangely silent. Normally our home was full of children's voices laughing, arguing or debating some issue or other. But today was different. I opened the door and saw the children all hugging their mother on the sofa. They were all crying.

"Lee Po is dead," said Amy through her tears.

I saw the letter on the coffee table and picked it up. As I read, I felt like a blind man stumbling down an endless and narrowing corridor from which there was no escape. In my heart I was suddenly a little boy again, the one who had sat on the wooden floor of an oxcart all those years ago watching my mother fade away. I closed my eyes and tried to remember my mother's face, but all I could see in my mind's eye was a faded shadow waving to me from a great distance. Time and space now separated us, the two unconquerable gulfs that no living man can cross. Even as I write these words my heart is full of a speechless sorrow I cannot express.

At supper that evening no one spoke. The children were all quiet. Belle needing to fill the silence switched our radio on to listen to the Redifusion station. Massenet's *Élégie* was playing.

I sat listening to the cello, remembering that time long ago when a small boy had watched his mother's face fade into the distance. Now there was a distance between us that no ship, plane or car could carry me across. The memory of her wordless farewell was too much for me. A wave of agony wracked my body and I went into the bedroom. Collapsing on the tiled floor, I finally broke down in choking, aching sobs.

The door opened. Looking up, I saw Belle and the children, framed by the sitting-room light behind them, watching me.

I wiped my face with my sleeve, opened my arms, and my children ran to me. I held them as close and as tight as I had ever done. All of us huddled together on the bathroom floor grieving for an old woman we all loved, whom we would never see again.

21

THE END AND THE BEGINNING

After my mother's death, we all tried to continue with life as best we could. I remained the manager of the Canton Trust & Commercial Bank in Hong Kong and busied myself with work. With each passing season the children grew, and soon it was time for Amy to graduate from the Maryknoll Convent School. My dream had been for all my children to go to university in the United States as I had done, but it wasn't possible. The war had wiped out all of our savings and the Communists had confiscated the land and home we owned in Canton. All we had was my monthly salary.

I desperately wanted Amy to have a university education and not simply rush into a marriage with the first boy who came along. I knew she dreamt of studying in the United States as well, but she didn't want me to worry when I broached the subject.

"No, Daddy, I would like to get a job first, if you don't mind," she said.

"Don't you want to go to the States, Amy?"

"Yes, very much," replied Amy kindly. "But I think I would like to wait for a little while longer until I'm ready."

I felt terrible. I wanted to be able to give her everything in the world, including an education, and here she was, being decent and understanding. She was a good girl, yet I felt I had failed her.

After graduation, Amy started looking for jobs as she said she would. Employment was tough in Hong Kong at that time because of the American Embargo Act on goods going into Communist territories. As a trading port, Hong Kong was suffering. But Amy was a trained steno-typist, and she eventually landed a job with Philippine Airlines. The manager in Hong Kong was called Mike Kendall, an old friend of mine. Amy was to start at $400 a month. She had been working there only two days when I asked how it was going.

"Oh, it's lovely," replied Amy. "We have the most swanky offices in town. And there are just the two of us, Mrs. Leong and myself. Guess what, Daddy? Mrs. Leong told me that every employee of our airline is entitled to a three-week leave to America, with round-trip fare all paid for, once we've completed a year of service! I am so looking forward to that trip to America, Daddy."

"Well, I'm certainly glad to hear that, Amy," I said, trying to share my daughter's joy. "If you'll work hard, be attentive to your duty, and be prompt at the office, undoubtedly you'll make that trip."

While Amy was dreaming of her trip to America, Hong Kong's economy was suffering and I saw little possibility of my family's financial predicament improving in the short term. Going to work at the bank each day, I tried to embrace routine, but I was restless and frustrated. I knew I was lucky to be employed, but I had always dreamt of more. I had come close to securing my family financially a couple of times, but circumstances had prevailed against me and we had lost everything each time. Here I was, approaching fifty, stuck being a wage slave, unable to fund my children's college dreams.

Belle did her best to cheer me up as my birthday arrived. She set up five tables for a feast at home to mark the occasion of my fiftieth year. I wasn't in a mood to celebrate, though. I became a grave man, trapped by circumstance and guilt. Belle saw how despondent I was and one Sunday morning she came to me with a suggestion, something she thought might cheer me up. She wanted to take me to see a fortune-teller.

"I know a blind palmist whom everybody says is uncanny," she said.

I was reluctant to go at first, but then thought, why not? Belle's enthusiasm warmed me to the idea. So that afternoon Belle and I went into the heart of the city, where the palmist lived. There were two people waiting in a small room to see him when we arrived. Our turn finally came.

"Your right palm on the table, please," requested the blind man.

I obeyed. Belle sat next to me, nervously hoping that the palmist would have good things to say about our future.

"You have a wonderful palm," the blind man began. "You have held many respectable positions, but were not able to save any money. You were, however, never in a desperate position, as there was always someone who would come to your rescue. You've thought it coincidence, but it wasn't. You have met many bad people, Mr. Lee. But you have also met angels. You do not know it, but you have always been a rich man, although you have not always chosen to see it. I have a message for you. Be grateful for what you already have, a home full of love and people who love you, and you will have found true happiness."

A few weeks later I was helping Amy apply for her passport in preparation for her trip abroad. It was due to take place some time in August, but Amy preferred to postpone it until September when the climate in San Francisco would be a little cooler. Belle was pushing the dressmakers to have all of Amy's dresses ready on time and rushing about town picking up presents for relatives in California.

Her departure date finally came, September 3, 1952. The whole family traveled with Amy to the airline's Kowloon office in the Peninsula Hotel. After we waited at the hotel for about an hour, an airline ground hostess notified the departing passengers that the time had come to board the airline's private bus to take them to the airport. My eldest daughter was about to leave us.

Amy hugged everybody. I could see that she was crying at the thought of leaving us all behind. As she climbed onto the bus, she smiled at me. The bus door closed behind her. Then, suddenly, she was gone.

Belle felt terribly lonely when we got home later. She was happy that her daughter had the opportunity to see the world, but she also knew that the world would change her daughter. Belle said that when Amy got on that bus, she was saying goodbye to her child in a far deeper sense than just saying farewell.

Three days later, we received a cable from Amy:

ARRIVED FRISCO STAYING WITH UNCLE HOPE
EVERYTHING ALL RIGHT LOVE AMY.

Many letters came from Amy over the following days, which I would read to the family over supper. They were comforting, since we all missed her, but I sensed that the emotional texture of my much-loved little family's world was changing. With every new letter, like the sonatas and operas I loved to listen to, I could now detect the faint whisper of new themes and voices emerging. It was true of all the children: four new melodies were breaking through all that had been, evolving from the notes and patterns we had designed for them, each becoming separate and distinct, emerging as its own. My children were growing up. They were leaving the world that I had built for them far behind.

If there is anything that is certain in life, it is this. Time doesn't always heal. Not really. I know they say it does, but that is not true. What time does is trick you into believing that you have healed, that the hurt of a great loss has lessened. But a single word, a note of a song, a fragrance, a knife point of dawn light across an empty room, any one of these things will take you back to *that* one moment you have never truly forgotten. These small things are the agents of memory. They are the sharp needle points piercing the living fabric of your life.

Life, my children, isn't linear where the heart is concerned. It is filled with invisible threads that reach out from your past and into your future. These threads connect every second we have lived and breathed. As your own lives move forward and as the decades pass the more of these threads are cast. Your task is to weave them into a tapestry, one that tells the story of the time we shared.

I hope that as a father I was a good one. I hope I gave you enough inspiration, hope and love to carry you through into the final years of your own lives. It hurts me to think that I will not be there to comfort you through the uncertainty and fear that old age will undoubtedly bring. That's why this manuscript is important. I want it to be a gentle golden thread of memory to connect us, to remind you that you, my children, were, and always will be, loved. The love I have for you is a single thread of shimmering, unbreakable certainty. One that was created with your first breath in this world and one that will be linked to you until your last. When the time comes for your own story to end, do not be afraid, my little ones. At that moment, you will see that thread of certain light. It will give you the courage to step through that last doorway and then guide you home to me.

Amy, Huey, Rudy and Yvonne, my children.
Good night and God bless, until we meet again.
I love you still.
Dad

Bo and Stephen arrive in California, 1956

EPILOGUE

March 1, 2012

My dear Dad, "Deh-Deh,"
There can be no words, sentences or chapters in a book that will sufficiently express my heartfelt love, gratitude, respect and admiration for you and the sacrifices you made for Amy, Rudy, Yvonne and me as children.

Rudy sadly died of cancer a few years ago and didn't live to see your story published. Amy, Yvonne and I are now in our seventies and eighties and not a day goes by without us thinking about you, Rudy and Mummy.

I personally regret that I missed the opportunity to tell you how proud I was of you and how fortunate I always felt to have had a father like you. When a man becomes a father, he needs a role model to guide him, and you were mine. If I have been only half as good a father to my three children as you were to me, then I will judge myself a success.

I also want to thank you for leaving behind this legacy of your writing, some of which has now been published here in this book. Since you left us, some forty years ago now, I have read and reread your words countless times. As each decade passed, as I grew and matured, I would always discover some new insight and inspiration in them.

Now, in the latter stages of my own life, your voice is more important to me than ever before. It not only provides comfort, it has made me realize that the highest aspiration a man can have is to be a gentleman, and you, Deh-Deh, were the gentlest of men. Quiet, reserved and watchful, yet full of deep feeling and sensitivity and far-sighted enough to know that your "little ones" would still need you long after you had gone. Daddy, you found a way to reach out across time to your children, and for that I thank you.

Someone told me once that time can wither the strong; it can reduce empires to dust and the ideologies of mankind to fragments of history. They said that nothing can stand against time. I have to disagree. Kindness and compassion can. Your story, Deh-Deh, is testament to that.

I hope that you are proud of the people we became.
We were, and still are, very proud of you.
We love you and Mummy still.
Huey

AFTERWORD

The following notes drawn from Huey Lee's recollections and anecdotes provide a snapshot view of the life of the Lee family from their emigration to the United States in 1955 up until Stephen's death on April 25, 1970.

On December 18, 1955, the Lee family sailed to the United States on board the SS *President Wilson*. They could only afford Third Class tickets, so they slept in cramped double-decker bunk beds below decks and passed their days playing ping-pong and chatting with the other passengers, many of whom were students traveling to the US to study. After four days at sea the ship docked at Osaka, Japan.

Despite everything the Lee family had lived through, they resolved to go ashore and see something of Japan. By chance, they befriended a Japanese woman on board the liner, the wife of an American serviceman, on her way to Chicago to meet her husband. When she heard that the Lees planned to visit Osaka, she offered to be their unofficial guide. Hiring a taxi for the day, the family saw Japan for the first time, and what struck them most was how courteous its people were. It was a stark contrast to the Japanese soldiers they had encountered during the war.

Leaving Osaka, the liner headed to Tokyo. Being old enough to venture out on their own, Huey and Rudy were given permission to go ashore and explore. Unfortunately, the Japanese lady who had accompanied the family around Osaka had a prior engagement and couldn't accompany the young men. Undaunted, Huey and Rudy hired a taxi as they'd done before and asked the driver to show them the sights. There was clearly something lost in translation, because the taxi driver immediately drove the boys to Tokyo's red-light district, believing this was the only destination that two young men in the first flush of their manhood would be interested in. Rudy and Huey had lived through a world war, but the throng of heavily made-up women who immediately surrounded their taxi touting for business left them terrified. They locked the taxi doors and refused to get out. Not sure what to do with his shell-shocked passengers, the perplexed taxi driver drove the young men back to the port, where they sheepishly tried to explain to their father the reason for the shortest tour of Tokyo in history.

After twelve days at sea since Hong Kong, the *President*

Wilson finally arrived in Honolulu on Christmas Eve, 1955. Stephen and the family were greeted by one of General Wong's daughters at the dockside and given a special car tour of Honolulu before being treated to a top Chinese restaurant and a special meal held in their honor.

Leaving Honolulu, the Lee family embarked on the last leg of the trip to San Francisco. It was a four-day trip and sailing was fine until two days into the journey when a fierce storm whipped up. The ship was battered by twenty-foot waves and all the passengers on board were violently sick, with the notable exception of Huey and Rudy. The young men took full advantage of the situation and ate for the entire family in the empty dining room.

As the liner approached San Francisco, the captain gave permission for the Third Class passengers to come up onto the upper deck so they could watch the approach to the Golden Gate Bridge. Huey recalls seeing the bridge draw near and wondering whether he would be able to cope with the discrimination his own father had faced during his time in the United States.

Stephen and his family were among the first wave of refugees from Communist China allowed into the United States. The family was given priority because Stephen had been brought up and educated in America. Getting to America wasn't without its problems for Stephen, though. Because Huey was nearly twenty-one, it was a race against time to get his visa approved before this vital birthday.

If Stephen missed the deadline, Huey wouldn't be allowed to come with the family and would have to remain in Hong Kong. It was touch and go, but the visa was finally granted with a few days to spare.

The family had braced themselves for an intensive interrogation by an immigration officer, but all they were asked were their names, their parents' names and whether they had accommodations arranged. It was something of an anticlimax after all the preparation Stephen had made them endure in anticipation of the immigration interview. Stephen and his family were admitted into the United States on January 4, 1956.

Amy was already living and studying in America, and she greeted the family with Sam Leong at the port. Uncle Sam, as Huey calls him, was the Lee family's visa sponsor. He ran a grocery store in San Leandro, a small town outside of Oakland, and had a home there. The plan was to stay with Uncle Sam until Stephen got a job and could move the family into a place of their own.

The Lee family shared the San Leandro house with Uncle Sam's second wife and his children. The families would remain close for years afterwards and become further entwined when Sam's two sons married Amy and Yvonne.

Stephen and the family stayed with Uncle Sam for three months whilst the children adapted to life in America. Huey remembers that they spent hours sitting and watching television, trying to understand the culture and customs.

Amy, who was studying at San Francisco State College, was living in San Francisco in an apartment complex called the Golden Gate Girls' Dormitory, a special facility set up to cater to single girls on low incomes. She had already begun to carve a life out for herself in California.

After three months, Stephen, who didn't want to overstay the family's welcome at Uncle Sam's, found a small apartment behind a relative's house. The new apartment, situated on Fourteenth Street in downtown Oakland, had a single bedroom with a compact living area. Huey and Rudy slept in the sitting room while Yvonne shared her parents' bedroom.

As both Rudy and Huey had graduated from high school in Hong Kong, they planned to continue their education in America. As a registered permanent resident in California, Stephen could have the boys' school tuition paid by the state, but it came with a catch: they would also be eligible for the draft.

When they tried to enroll at Oakland City College, Huey and Rudy were given an aptitude examination that covered math and English, both written and spoken. They passed math with perfect scores but both failed in their written English. The examiner's report said they couldn't spell properly. When the results were challenged, it became clear that Rudy and Huey, who had learned British English, not American, had completed their papers using British spellings. The examiner was unmoved by this straightforward explanation, and the school, without further review or the application of common sense, put them both into remedial English. It was particularly frustrating for Huey, who loved to read Dickens and understood all the British colloquialisms, to find himself sitting in a class of people learning their ABCs.

There were very few foreign students at Oakland City College back in 1956; Huey and Rudy were objects of fascination for many and often found themselves asked to give informal talks about life in China. Among the students Huey made friends with were a number of veterans who had just returned from the Korean War. Many of these young men were deeply traumatized by their experience in Korea and expressed it in various quirks of manner and speech. One veteran found it impossible to sit in his seat during class, opting to crouch on his seat instead. Most students chose to ignore these quirks, understanding something of what these young men had been through. Having lived through a war and seen its horrors firsthand, Huey in particular empathized with the returning soldiers. He found the veterans hard-working, decent and accepting of him. On the whole, they didn't seem to have the racial hangups other people had; it was as though the experience they had gone through had made things like race matter less. They were happy to simply be alive and, like Huey and Rudy, they just wanted to better their lives and move forward.

As a full-time student Huey was able to delay the draft, but it was only a matter of time. Nine months after they'd arrived in the United States, the expected letter finally came, asking him to report to the draft office.

Virtually since Stephen had stepped off the liner he had been trying to find employment in the banking sector, but after a vigorous letter-writing campaign, which gleaned a number of interviews, he found himself consistently rejected. He thought that his considerable experience in the industry and his extensive qualifications would allow him to break into the mainly white-run profession. He was very wrong. Despite having been a professor teaching finance to students, being widely published in American accountancy journals and having years of solid commercial banking experience, he hit a brick wall. Over and over he reached the interview stage only to be told that he was either "overqualified" or "not what we're looking for." When it was clear he wouldn't be given the job, Stephen would always offer to come and work for the bank for free for a month to prove his worth. He didn't care what job they gave to him; he had experience in both retail and commercial banking and could turn his hand to either. Stephen challenged the interviewers to simply let him come to work and prove his worth and experience. These offers were rejected out of hand. Sitting outside of interview rooms, he was the only non-white candidate for most jobs, and on one occasion the interviewer even refused to see him when it became clear he was Chinese.

After six months of unemployment, Stephen's savings were almost at an end and he desperately needed an income. Without a job on the horizon, he decided to approach his cousins and ask for help. He was prepared to do anything to support his family. That's when a relative stepped in and offered to lend Stephen $10,000 to start up a grocery store in Oakland.

Without any other option, Stephen accepted the loan. He gave up all thought of becoming a banker again and accepted his lot as a grocer. It was a long way from the Canton Trust Company and a tough choice for a proud man. The new grocery store was called Steve's Market and was located on Fortieth Street and Grove.

It was physically hard work for Stephen. He'd get up with Huey and Rudy at 4 a.m. each day to go to the market to buy fresh vegetables to stock the store. Huey and Rudy would then stack the shelves and fill the storeroom until it was time for them to go to class at 8 a.m. It was a long and tiring day. On the weekends, all the Lee children, including Amy, would band together to run the store to give their parents the chance of a break.

The grocery had a meat counter, and one of Stephen's many tasks was to learn how to be a butcher so they could stock it. The sight of his exhausted father bent beneath the weight of heavy slabs of meat as he shifted them from the cold room to be cut up at the meat counter hurt Huey deeply. He knew his father regarded being reduced to a grocer as a personal failure and wished he could do more for his family than simply provide meals and a roof over their heads. It was a humiliation after all he had achieved academically, all his experience and his qualifications. Despite everything, Stephen hid his feelings from his family and never complained; when asked, he would say that he was simply happy to support his family.

Needing to be nearer the store, Stephen decided to rent an apartment on Fifty-Third Street and invested some savings in a used 1952 Chevrolet to transport produce and the family. The apartment was on the second floor and comprised three bedrooms, a living room and a kitchen. It wasn't a palace, but Stephen was pleased to have provided a home for his family he wasn't ashamed to live in.

A highlight of Stephen's life came when Amy enrolled in the University of California at Berkeley, the same college that he had graduated from in the 1920s.

Around the time Yvonne graduated from Oakland High School, Huey was busy writing to a girl he had fallen in love with in Hong Kong, May Chan. Huey was desperate for May to come to California and study there so they could be together. By 1958, May had finished high school in Hong Kong with top grades and wrote to tell Huey she was ready to apply to colleges in the US if she could get a scholarship.

While Huey was serving in the US Army, the lease on Steve's Market came up and the landlord refused to renew it. This left Stephen desperately searching for a replacement store. He finally found a new location on Twenty-Third Avenue in Oakland. The new store came with an apartment upstairs and one in back.

As they settled into the new store, Amy married Sam

Leong's son Jenkin. It wasn't long before they announced that they were expecting, and as Amy was keen to be close to her mother, she moved into the apartment above the new store. Amy and Jenkin would go on to have three daughters—Cindy, June and Noreen—and a son, Kenneth.

Meanwhile, Huey had received word that May Chan, with Amy's help, had found an opening at a Catholic school called Holy Name College in the Oakland Hills. All she needed was a sponsor to come to United States. As Stephen had a business in Oakland, he was in a position to do this, and after various letters and forms had been filled out, May's status was approved. Huey had been saving his Army pay and had planned on giving it to his parents to help them, but Stephen insisted that his son use the money to ensure that May came to the United States.

Not long afterwards, Stephen spotted an opportunity when the owners of a store on Fourteenth Avenue near Lake Merrit decided to retire. It was a better location and came with a delivery truck. This was to be the last Steve's Market.

Stephen's children, with his encouragement, all did well academically. Yvonne was admitted to the University of California, while Rudy graduated with a degree in biological science from San Jose State College and accepted a position at the California State Department of Public Health. On September 23,1961, Huey and May finally got married in Oakland while both of them were still in school. Huey eventually graduated from San Jose State University with a degree in electrical engineering and joined Lockheed Aerospace Corporation in Sunnyvale, California, as an engineer. With their lives taking shape, Huey and May would add three more children, Melinda, Kevin and Julianne, to the expanding Lee family. Rudy fell in love with a girl called Daisy, and the couple would welcome a daughter called Annabel into their lives, while Yvonne married Sam Leong's younger son, Bing, and the marriage was blessed with a daughter called Nicole.

Concerned for their father's health after he was diagnosed with cancer of the nose and throat, Amy, Huey, Rudy and Yvonne sat Stephen and Belle down and persuaded them to retire from the grocery store. Reluctantly, Stephen agreed. His condition deteriorated, and after a long illness he passed away on April 25, 1970. His ashes were buried in Mountain View Cemetery in Oakland. A small headstone marks the plot.

Belle survived Stephen and lived quietly in California until her death in 2001.

ACKNOWLEDGMENTS

First, I would like to thank my wife, Julianne Lee, for her patience, love and support; without her none of this would have been possible. Second, I would like to thank Amy, Huey, Yvonne and Daisy for entrusting me with Stephen Jin-Nom Lee's manuscript. It is through them, their children and grandchildren that Stephen and Belle's legacy lives on and the story continues.

Thanks go to my parents, John and Irene Webster, and Julianne's parents, Huey and May Lee, for their consistent encouragement, love and help. The Lee-Leong book committee, comprising Julianne, Nicole, Annabel and Kenneth, is also due recognition for marshaling the extended families together and pushing the project forward. I would also like to say thank you to Kevin Lee and Melinda Lee and everyone else who rushed contracts around the Bay Area.

Nicole Leong also comes in for a special note of gratitude for putting together the sample artwork that was used at the London Book Fair; it was very last-minute and she did an amazing job.

Angela Donovan is due a big hug from me for her quiet and insightful support of this project. Note to Angela: *Canton Elegy* was a *wish* made in 1955 and patiently waited all this time to come into being. I would also like to thank my literary agent, Susan Mears, for her support and belief in Stephen Jin-Nom Lee's book. I would like to thank Anne Barthel for her brilliant editing of the manuscript; it was a pleasure working with you. Finally, I would like to thank, on behalf of the late Stephen Jin-Nom Lee and myself, everyone at Watkins for their belief in *Canton Elegy*. The book has found its way home at last.

ABOUT THE AUTHOR

Stephen Jin-Nom Lee was born on November 27, 1902, in the village of Dai Waan in Zhongshan near Guangzhou, China. He died in 1970, leaving behind the *Canton Elegy* manuscript about his life in China and America. The manuscript charts his family's epic struggle for survival in the face of war, starvation, corruption and poverty.

Lee's father died shortly after he was born, and at eight years old he was sent to live in America by his grandfather. The price for his education was that his mother would remain in China and care for his grandmother. Lee remained in California until after he had graduated with a degree in economics from the University of California at Berkeley. Then, unable to secure employment in California due to racism in the 1920s, he burned his American papers and returned to a China on the verge of civil war. Lee's accountancy skills led him to become the comptroller of the Chinese Air Force with the rank of full colonel. Leaving the military, Lee became a banker and then a professor teaching finance. He married Lum Bo King, "Belle," in Canton and together they raised four children: Amy, Huey, Rudy and Yvonne.

The Lee family life was set against the backdrop of a war-torn China. They lived through the Chinese civil war, the Second Sino–Japanese War, the Second World War, and the Cultural Revolution. Having survived war, poverty and social upheaval, Lee moved his family to California anxious for peace and quietly resumed life in Berkeley in 1956. He is survived by nine grandchildren and sixteen great-grandchildren.

ABOUT THE CO-AUTHOR

Howard Webster is a published photographer, writer and film director. He spent the early years of his life living between Nigeria and England. He graduated from Durham University and lives in London. He is married to Stephen Jin-Nom Lee's granddaughter Julianne Lee and is the father of twins, Alexandra and Frederick.